Essential
Menorca

by Tony Kelly

Tony Kelly took up travel writing after
teaching English in Sudan and China.
He writes regularly for newspapers and
magazines, specialising in walking and the
outdoors. When not travelling he lives on
a farm in eastern England with his wife
and young son. He is the author of
AA *Essential Mallorca*.

AA Publishing

Above: *Plaça des Born, Ciutadella*

Page 1: *the beach at Cala Macarelleta*

Page 5a: *boats at Fornells*
5b: *meditating at Cala d'Alcaufar*

Page15a: *Naveta des Tudons*
15b: *sailing near Fornells*

Page 27a: *Cala Macarelleta*
27b: *a roundabout with a difference, outside Ciutadella*

Page 91a: *chairs at Binimel-là*
91b: *children playing in Es Castell*

Page 117a: *Ciutadella lleyway*
17b: *catching a siesta in laça des Born*

d out more about
Publishing and the
e range of services
AA provides by
ng our Web site at
v.theaa.co.uk

Written by Tony Kelly

Edited, designed and produced by AA Publishing.
© The Automobile Association 1998
Maps © The Automobile Association 1998

Distributed in the United Kingdom by AA Publishing,
Norfolk House, Priestley Road, Basingstoke, Hampshire,
RG24 9NY.

A CIP catalogue record for this book is available from the
British Library.

ISBN 0 7495 1632 1

The Automobile Association retains the copyright in the
original edition © 1998 and in all subsequent editions,
reprints and amendments.

All rights reserved. No part of this publication may be
reproduced, stored in a retrieval system, or transmitted in
any form or by any means – electronic, photocopying,
recording or otherwise – unless the written permission of
the publishers has been obtained beforehand. This book
may not be sold, resold, hired out or otherwise disposed of
by way of trade in any form of binding or cover other than
that in which it is published, without the prior consent of
the publisher.

The contents of this publication are believed correct at
the time of printing. Nevertheless, the publishers cannot
be held responsible for any errors or omissions or for
changes in the details given in this guide or for the
consequences of any reliance on the information provided
by the same. Assessments of attractions, hotels,
restaurants and so forth are based upon the author's own
experience and, therefore, descriptions given in this guide
necessarily contain an element of subjective opinion which
may not reflect the publisher's opinion or dictate a reader's
own experience on another occasion.

We have tried to ensure accuracy in this guide, but
things do change and we would be grateful if readers
would advise us of any inaccuracies they may encounter.

Published by AA Publishing, a trading name of Automobile
Association Developments Limited, whose registered
office is Norfolk House, Priestley Road, Basingstoke,
Hampshire, RG24 9NY.
Registered number 1878835.

Colour separation: BTB Digital Imaging Ltd,
Whitchurch, Hampshire

Printed and bound in Italy by Printers Trento srl

Contents

About this Book

KEY TO SYMBOLS

Throughout the guide a few straightforward symbols are used to denote the following categories:

✚ map reference to the maps in the What to See section

✉ address

☎ telephone number

◷ opening times

🍴 restaurant or café on premises or near by

Ⓜ nearest underground train station

🚌 nearest bus/tram route

🚆 nearest overground train station

⛴ nearest ferry stop

♿ facilities for visitors with disabilities

✋ admission charge

↔ other places of interest near by

❓ other practical information

➤ indicates the page where you will find a fuller description

---

Essential *Menorca* is divided into five sections to cover the most important aspects of your visit to Menorca.

Viewing Menorca pages 5–14
An introduction to Menorca by the author.
   Menorca's Features
   Essence of Menorca
   The Shaping of Menorca
   Peace and Quiet
   Menorca's Famous

Top Ten pages 15–26
The author's choice of the Top Ten places to see in Menorca, each with practical information.

What to See pages 27–90
The main areas of Menorca, each with its own brief introduction and an alphabetical listing of the main attractions.
   Practical information
   Snippets of 'Did You Know…' information
   5 suggested walks
   3 suggested tours
   2 features

Where To... pages 91–116
Detailed listings of the best places to eat, stay, shop, take the children and be entertained.

Practical Matters pages 117–24
A highly visual section containing essential travel information.

Maps
All map references are to the individual maps found in the What to See section of this guide.
For example, Fornells has the reference
✚ 29D4 – indicating the page on which the map is located and the grid square in which the village is to be found. A list of the maps that have been used in this travel guide can be found in the index.

Prices
Where appropriate, an indication of the cost of an establishment is given by
£ signs:
£££ denotes higher prices, **££** denotes average prices, while **£** denotes lower charges.

Star Ratings
Most of the places described in this book have been given a separate rating:

✪✪✪   Do not miss
✪✪   Highly recommended
✪   Worth seeing

Viewing
Menorca

Tony Kelly's Menorca

Stones and Wind

Mario Verdaguer called his novel about Menorca *Stones and Wind*, and it is easy to see why. The stones are everywhere, from prehistoric burial chambers to modern barns, often side by side in the same field. As for wind, of eight distinct named winds, the fiercest and most common is the *tramuntana*, the north wind which blows for around 150 days a year.

Even on the most crowded beaches you are never far from an unspoilt cove, such as this one at Cala Pregonda

'Wind and stones', 'a rock strewn with earth' – Menorca has been called many things. 'The blue and white island', for the clarity of its light and the contrasts between dazzling white houses and a turquoise sea. 'An open-air museum', for its megalithic monuments – piles of ancient stones which blend into the modern landscape. Sometimes it is difficult to know where the clichés end and the truth begins.

Romans and Byzantines, British and Spanish colonists have all left their mark; even the tourist invasion since the 1960s has created its own monuments. But the biggest influence on Menorca remains what it has always been – the sea.

There are plenty of crowded beach resorts, indistinguishable from their equivalents elsewhere; yet at the same time you find peaceful coves, where pine-clad rocks surround arcs of fine sand. Out of season you might have one of these beaches to yourself. Yourself and the sharp north wind.

The cities at either end of the island personify Menorca's contrasts. Georgian Maó, the colonial capital, is a place of civil servants and naval officers, protected by one of the world's great harbours. Catalan Ciutadella, all aristocratic mansions and Gothic churches, is just 45km away but feels like another world. Between them is a rural landscape of meadows, cattle and drystone walls, punctuated by solid market towns and a gentle range of hills.

Don't fool yourself; you would not be in Menorca if it wasn't for sun, sea and sand. But stick to the beach for a fortnight and you will never know what else you are missing.

Menorca's Features

Geography and Landscape
• Menorca is the second largest of the Balearic Islands, a group that includes Mallorca, Ibiza and Formentera.
• Menorca lies 225km southeast of Barcelona at the eastern extremity of Spain.
• Menorca measures 53km from east to west and 23km from north to south at its widest point.
• Menorca has 220km of coastline, with more beaches than all the other Balearic Islands put together.
• The highest mountain is Monte Toro (358m).
• Menorca has at least 1,000 prehistoric monuments and 15,000km of drystone walls.

Language
Most people speak Menorquín, which is a dialect of Catalan. Since 1983 Catalan and Castilian Spanish have both enjoyed official status on Menorca, but there has been a trend towards the revival of Catalan, especially in place-names. Menorquín contains a number of words inherited during the 18th-century British occupation – examples include *grevi* (gravy) and *winder* (a sash window).

Climate
• Menorca has an average daily maximum temperature of 20.3°C, rising to 28°C in July and falling to 14°C in January. Menorca has an average of 315 sunny days a year.
• Menorca is the wettest of the Balearic Islands; the rainy season is from October to April.

People
• Menorca has a population of 66,000, of whom around 24,000 live in Maó and 21,000 in Ciutadella.

Tourism
• In 1950 Menorca had 200 hotel rooms; by 1995 it had 40,000 in hotels and apartments.
• Menorca received 8,000 tourists in 1960, 56,000 in 1970, 200,000 in 1980 and 800,000 in 1995. In 1995, 67 per cent of visitors were British, 13 per cent were German and 10 per cent were from mainland Spain.
• In 1995, 90 per cent of tourists arrived between May and September and 99.5 per cent between April and October.

The countryside is dotted with ancient monuments, like this 6th-century church at Torelló

Essence of Menorca

Menorca is the quiet one of the Balearics. Mallorca may be larger, Ibiza may be brasher, but Menorca remains calm and dignified, confident of its own charms.

The wild olive trees of the north coast, bent into shape by the *tramuntana*, are symbolic of a people and an island shaped by history and a rugged landscape. Numerous invasions have not changed the Menorcan character – courteous and welcoming to strangers, yet self-sufficient and fiercely independent. Tourism has brought many benefits, but the Menorcans have not let themselves get carried away. The impression you get is of an island at ease with itself.

Arenal d'en Castell (below) and modern sculpture in Maó

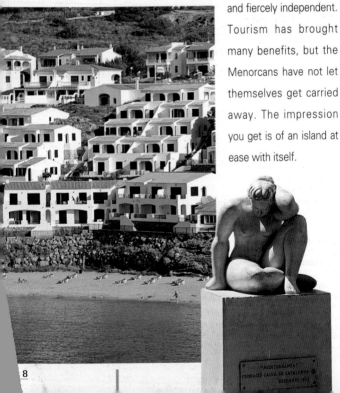

THE **10** ESSENTIALS

*If you only have a short time to visit the island,
or would like to get a really complete picture of it,
here are the essentials:*

• **Take a boat trip** around Maó harbour (▶ 23), then stroll along the waterfront for a drink in Cala Figuera (▶ 33).

• **Make the pilgrimage** – on foot or by car – to Monte Toro (▶ 20), the hilltop convent at the centre of the island.

Sun, sea and sand – the Mediterranean dream

• **Wander the back streets** of Ciutadella, where every other house is the palace of a noble family, with hidden architectural details and coats of arms above the door (▶ 38–44).

• **Have lunch by the harbour** at Fornells (▶ 18) – *caldereta de langosta* (▶ 98) if you can afford it.

• **Walk to a remote beach** that cannot be reached by car – take a picnic and plenty of water, and settle down to your own private view.

• **Seek out** some of Menorca's prehistoric sites and try to unravel the mystery of the *taulas* (▶ 13).

• **Go to the trotting races** in Maó or Ciutadella at weekends (▶ 113), the best place to see Menorcans indulge their passion for horses.

• **Find out where** there is a festival going on (▶ 116) and drop everything to get there – especially if it is the Festa de Sant Joan in Ciutadella.

• **Try some Mahón cheese** (▶ 55), then buy some to take home.

• **Lie on the beach** soaking up the sun – everyone else does it at least once. But don't forget your sunblock.

The traffic-free streets in the centre of Maó are home to some of the smartest shops on Menorca

The Shaping of Menorca

About 100 million years ago
Menorca is formed by a geological fusion between fragments of continental Europe and Andalusia.

2,000–123 BC
The Talaiotic period produces burial caves, *navetas* and large settlements with *talaiots* and *taulas*.

400 BC
Carthaginian invaders enlist Balearic slingshot throwers to fight in the Punic Wars; they are paid in wine and women.

123 BC
Roman conquest; Menorca is named *Balearis Minor*. Christianity is introduced, towns are established at Maó, Ciutadella and Sanitja, and a fort is built on Santa Agueda.

AD 533
After a century of Vandal rule, Menorca becomes part of the Byzantine Empire.

902
The Balearic Islands enter the Caliphate of Córdoba, under Islamic rule. Ciutadella, Menorca's second town, becomes Medina Minurka.

Pirate Barbarossa – his name means 'red beard'

1229
Jaume I of Aragón conquers Mallorca. The Arab rulers agree to become his vassals, paying an annual tribute in wheat, cattle and lard.

1287
Alfonso III of Aragón lands at Maó and the Moors surrender. Christianity is restored. Alfonso divides Menorca up among his followers but dies in 1291 aged 25. Menorca is ruled by the kings of Mallorca and Catalan becomes the main language.

1349
The kingdom of Mallorca comes to an end and Menorca is incorporated into Aragón.

1492
Aragón unites with Castile and Granada to create modern Spain.

1535
The Turkish pirate Barbarossa attacks Maó; more than half the population are killed or enslaved.

1554
Construction of Fort Sant Felip.

1558
A Turkish raid on Ciutadella destroys most of the city.

17th century
The British gain treaty rights to the use of Port de Maó. British influence on Menorca grows and Maó becomes the main city.

1708
The British occupy Menorca in the name of Charles, Archduke of Austria.

1713
The Treaty of Utrecht confirms British rule. The capital is moved to Maó and a new road is constructed across the island.

1756
The Battle of Menorca ends in a French victory and the execution of the British Admiral Byng.

1763–82
The second British occupation under the Treaty of Paris and the building of Georgetown (Es Castell).

1782–98
Menorca returns to Spanish rule. Fort Sant Felip is destroyed.

1798
The British retake Menorca without loss of life.

1802
The Treaty of Amiens returns Menorca to Spain.

1854
Opening of a steamer service between Maó and Barcelona.

1909
Formation of a Society for the Attraction of Foreigners.

1936–9
The Spanish Civil War – Menorca remains staunchly Republican and is the last part of Spain to surrender to General Franco. Under Franco's dictatorship (1939–75), the use of the Catalan language is forbidden.

1953
The first charter flight from England lands in Menorca.

1969
The opening of Sant Climent airport leads to the tourist boom.

1975
Death of Franco and restoration of the monarchy.

1978
A new constitution grants limited autonomy to the Spanish regions.

Admiral Byng pays the price for the loss of Menorca in 1756

1983
The Balearic Islands become an autonomous region, with Catalan as an official language.

1986
Spain joins the European Community.

1988
A new coastal law prohibits development within 100m of the sea.

1993
Menorca is declared a Unesco Biosphere Reserve; the aim is to protect the environment yet support traditional industries and tourism.

1994
The number of visitors reaches 800,000.

Peace & Quiet

Camí de Cavalls
This bridleway around the entire Menorcan coast was first built in the 14th century and restored during the brief French occupation of 1756–63. It has mostly fallen into disrepair; ambitious plans to reopen the whole route have met with opposition from landowners and to date only a small section in the southeast has been reconstructed.

The Roman road to the summit of Santa Agueda gives spectacular views across the island

It's not difficult to find peace and quiet in Menorca – sometimes it's harder to get away from it. Even on the most crowded beaches, you are never more than a short walk away from a peaceful cove, fragrant pine woods or tranquil countryside. Go in winter and you have the island to yourself; only one tourist in 200 arrives between November and March. You might have to wrap up against the north wind, but winter and, especially, early spring are beautiful on Menorca, and the mild sunny days are perfect for walking.

Walking

The paths and minor roads that have criss-crossed Menorca since Roman times provide gentle walking on largely flat land. The biggest challenges are the hills of Monte Toro (► 20) and Santa Agueda (► 84), but even these can be managed by anyone who is reasonably fit. Other good areas are the limestone gorges of the south (► 16) and the numerous coastal paths. Walking in the countryside, you encounter an attractive rural landscape of Moorish farmhouses, curved olive-wood gates, sheep-shelters and drystone walls. Rights of way are not always clear and forbidding notices are not uncommon, but a word with the farmer will often help. Remember to shut all gates and not to walk over crops. Wherever you are walking, it is a good idea to carry water and food and to protect yourself from the sun.

Prehistoric Sites

Menorca's prehistoric sites are among the most peaceful places on the island. Most are situated in the midst of farmland and reached along minor roads; although they are on private land visitors have free, open access.

The most common monuments include *navetas*, burial chambers shaped like an upturned boat, and *talaiots*, large circular structures used as both dwellings and watch-towers. Most mysterious of all are the *taulas*, T-shaped 'tables' which probably performed some religious ritual function.

Spring flowers in the Algendar Gorge and the S'Albufera nature reserve

Birds and Flowers

Menorca is a popular staging-post for thousands of migrant birds each spring and autumn, pausing for rest on their way across the Mediterranean. The best sites for birdwatching are the S'Albufera marshes (► 24), the southern gorges and the wilder coastal areas. Endemic species include red kites and booted eagles, as well as the brightly coloured bee-eater, which nests in sandbanks and dunes. The cliffs, fields, gorges and woods of Menorca become a riot of wild flowers in spring; among more than 200 species are several varieties of orchid, which come into flower between March and May.

Menorca's Famous

Mateu Orfila (1787–1853)
Dr Mateu Orfila was born in Menorca but became Dean of Medicine at the University of Paris. He is known as the founder of modern forensic medicine after his ground-breaking work on toxicology in 1813. A bust of Dr Orfila stands outside his house in Carrer Ses Moreres, Maó.

Joan Pons
The baritone Joan Pons was born in Ciutadella and still visits Menorca as often as time allows. Since 1980 he has performed at opera houses across Europe and North America, including La Scala in Milan, La Fenice in Venice, Covent Garden in London and the Metropolitan Opera in New York, where he has appeared with Placido Domingo and Luciano Pavarotti.

Alfonso III of Aragón (1265–91)

Although he only spent 45 days on Menorca, the hero of the Reconquest can take most of the credit for the influence of Catalan culture on the island. Succeeding to the throne at the age of 20, he immediately set about planning to capture Menorca. He sailed from the mainland in 1286, reached Maó in January 1287 and conquered Menorca two weeks later. During his brief stay he established a system of government that was to last for several centuries; he also distributed land among his followers, earning the nickname 'the Liberal' since he rarely refused a request. He was capable of cruelty as well – those Moors too poor to pay a ransom and too weak to work as slaves were simply taken out to sea and drowned. Alfonso died in Barcelona at the age of 25; his statue, donated by General Franco, stands in the Plaça Conquesta in Maó.

Sir Richard Kane (1662–1736)

When the British arrived in Menorca, resistance to Protestant rule and resentment at the duplicitous nature of their conquest meant there was a need for a governor who would win Menorcans' respect. Richard Kane fitted the bill perfectly. A Northern Irish soldier who had served in Flanders and Canada, he arrived in 1713 to become Lieutenant-Governor. His first act was to build a road across the island, from Maó to Ciutadella, financed by a tax on alcohol – much of the road stands today. At the same time he moved the capital from Ciutadella to Maó. He drained marshes, planted orchards, introduced Friesian cattle, and made daily visits to the market in Maó to check on prices and measures. Agricultural production increased by five times in 40 years. Kane remained in Menorca until his death and was buried in Fort Sant Felip. He is remembered on Menorca with affection and a monument to his achievements stands near the start of the Camí d'en Kane (➤ 87).

This monument to the memory of Sir Richard Kane was erected by the Menorcan people in 1973

Top Ten

1
Barranc d'Algendar
(Algendar Gorge)

A dramatic limestone gorge, buzzing with wildlife, which runs for 6km from Ferreries to the south coast.

✚ 28C3

🍴 At Cala Santa Galdana (£–££)

🚌 Buses from Maó, Ciutadella & Ferreries to Cala Santa Galdana in summer

↔ Cala Santa Galdana (► 64)

Menorca's *barrancs*, or gorges, are wild and lonely places, deep clefts formed over tens of thousands of years by the gradual erosion of the limestone plateau in the south.

The gorges attract a huge variety of wildlife – birds, butterflies, flowers. Kestrels and kites nestle among the rushes; you see herons, buzzards and booted eagles. Lizards sun themselves on the rocks and tortoises wade through the marshes. The combination of rainfall, humidity and protection from the wind produces a richness of vegetation rarely seen elsewhere.

Algendar Gorge is the most dramatic of all – and one of the easiest to explore. The stream flows throughout the year, opening out at Cala Santa Galdana (► 64) into a wide

The lush valley floor supports orchards and market gardens as well as a huge variety of wild flowers

river beside the beach. From here you can walk along its western side, where pine trees grow out of the cliffs at remarkable angles.

There is greater access, and more of a sense of peace, at the northern end. Take the minor road off the Maó–Ciutadella highway 100m west of the Cala Santa Galdana exit; when the tarmac runs out, walk down the lane to your right. After passing a white house hidden in the trees, you will enter a narrow valley where red kites circle overhead.

2
Cala Pregonda

A peaceful bay, backed by pine and tamarisk woods, in a remote and sheltered corner of the north coast.

+ 28C4

🍴 None

↔ Binimel-là (➤ 52)

Everyone has their own favourite Menorcan cove but the one factor they all have in common is that you cannot reach them by road. Approaching Cala Pregonda on foot, you wonder what all the fuss is about – surely a perfect cove cannot have concrete houses behind the beach? But sit against the dunes with your back to the houses, surrounded by wild flowers on a quiet day in spring or autumn, looking out beyond the shore to the sandstone rocks and beyond that to Cap de Cavallería (➤ 69), and you begin to feel the magic of this place.

An old Roman road runs from Santa Agueda (➤ 84), but the easiest approach is from Binimel-là (➤ 52). Take the whitewashed steps over the wall at the west end of Binimel-là beach, follow the track across salt flats and a pebbly cove, climb a small headland above the dunes, then drop down to the beach.

The water is crystal-clear, ideal for swimming, though you might have to navigate your way around yachts. A short distance out to sea is a rocky islet with its own sandy beach, just right for a couple of families. Near here is Es Prego, the sandstone outcrop said to resemble a hooded monk (*prego* means proclamation), carved into shape by the fierce north wind. And behind the beach are the pine woods, the best place to take a picnic if you want to escape the crowds – and the sun.

And the houses? They were put up before the restrictions on coastal development were introduced. Even such modest building would not be permitted today.

The first sight of Cala Pregonda as you approach on foot from Binimel-là

3
Fornells

✚ 29D4

🍴 Wide choice of
restaurants on the
quayside (££–£££)

🚌 Buses from Maó

↔ Cala Tirant (➤ 65)

❓ Festa de la Verge del
Carme – procession and
blessing of boats on 16
Jul; Festa de Sant Antoni
– patronal festival, fourth
weekend in Jul

Fornells – scenes from a fishing village

An attractive fishing village of low, whitewashed houses at the edge of a long, sheltered bay.

Fornells is everybody's idea of a Mediterranean fishing village – white-painted houses around a harbour bobbing with boats, restaurants on the waterfront along a palm-lined promenade. Nowadays, of course, tourism is more important than fishing, but there is still a fishing industry here and the fish in the restaurants is genuinely local and fresh. Fornells is known above all for its spiny lobsters, the essential ingredient in a *caldereta de langosta* (➤ 98). King Juan Carlos of Spain sails over regularly from Mallorca just to eat lobster at Fornells.

The village is built on the west side of the Bay of Fornells, close to the open sea. The natural harbour is 5km in length, similar to that at Maó but shallower. The commander of the first British invasion force to Menorca wrote to his superiors that Maó and Fornells were the two best ports in the Mediterranean.

Founded to defend the north coast against pirate ships, Fornells grew in importance in the 17th century with the building of Castell Sant Antoni, modelled on Fort Sant Felip (➤ 76). The castle ruins stand beside the sea, facing a small island crowned by a watchtower. A path from here, by the water's edge, leads to the cape, where there is a lighthouse, a small rock shrine, and another watchtower. Walk right inside the tower to experience what would once have been the view of approaching invaders.

But most visitors don't go to Fornells for history. They go to soak up its simple beauty, to walk beside the quay then choose a harbourside restaurant to enjoy the freshest fish possible.

4
Monte Toro

✚ 29D3

☎ 37 50 60

🍴 Café (£)

✋ Free

↔ Es Mercadal (► 72)

❓ First Sun in May – blessing of the fields

The spiritual and physical high point of Menorca – a hilltop convent right at the centre of the island.

Menorca's highest mountain (358m) is crowned by a convent which has become an important centre of pilgrimage. Its name almost certainly derives from *al-tor*, Arabic for 'highest mountain', despite the local legend about a bull (*toro* in Spanish) who discovered a statue of the Virgin in a cleft in the rock.

Get there by driving or walking the twisting 3km road from Es Mercadal; an alternative approach on foot is to follow the track between two white posts at the entrance to San Carlos farm, 1km out of Es Mercadal on the Camí d'en Kane (► 87). The simple courtyard is peaceful and attractive – an old well, an olive tree, a 16th-century stone tower, a low white-washed refectory. You enter the church through a pretty

A large statue of Christ welcomes weary pilgrims arriving at the summit of Monte Toro

porch with several arches and dozens of potted plants. Even when you get inside the 17th-century Renaissance church, there is little adornment – a plain white dome, tapestries on the walls, a 1943 altarpiece with a statue of the Virgin with the legendary bull at her feet. This is La Verge del Toro, the chief focus of pilgrimage. Mass is said here at 11AM each Sunday and the bishop holds a service each May to bless the island's fields.

From the terrace and car park there are sea views on all four sides. Look down from the terrace over neat vegetable and herb gardens which are tended by the community of nuns who still live on Monte Toro.

5
Naveta des Tudons

The oldest roofed building in Spain – a Bronze Age burial chamber recently restored to its former glory.

Of all the prehistoric monuments on Menorca, this is probably the most visited. Until the 1950s it was dishevelled and overgrown; for centuries it had been used as a cattle-shed but was fully restored in 1959–60 and again in 1975.

The word *naveta* describes a burial chamber, built in the shape of an upturned boat. Most are horseshoe-shaped in design, with a low, narrow entrance at the straight end and a small ante-chamber leading into the main burial chamber. Some, like this, were built on two storeys; the bodies were left to decompose upstairs and the bones were subsequently transferred to the ground floor ossuary. Excavations in the 1950s revealed at least 100 corpses in Naveta des Tudons, some with bronze bracelets still around their arm-bones.

 28B4

 On Maó–Ciutadella road, 4km from Ciutadella

 Free access

None

 Torre Llafuda (➤ 89)

Navetas are unique to Menorca – of around 45 remaining, this is in the best condition. It is 14m long, 6m wide and around 4m high. Although a notice warns you not to disturb the stones by climbing, you can enter the *naveta* on hands and knees for a close look at the main chamber, supported by stone columns. You may even think you can smell the bones.

Because it is on the main road so close to Ciutadella, Naveta des Tudons attracts a large number of visitors. Come here early in the morning or late in the afternoon to catch some of the atmosphere and history of this place.

Menorca's Bronze Age burial chambers were built using limestone from local quarries

6
Plaça des Born, Ciutadella

🕇 28A4

🍴 Wide choice of restaurants & bars (£–££)

🚌 Buses from west coast resorts to Plaça de S'Esplanada in summer; buses from Maó arrive 5 minutes' walk away

↔ Ciutadella (➤ 38)

❓ Festa de Sant Joan, 23–4 Jun

Open-air cafés and elegant 19th-century buildings – one of the finest city squares in Spain.

During the Fascist era this square at the heart of Ciutadella was renamed after General Franco, but everyone continued to call it 'es Born'. The word *born* means parade-ground – the square was used for jousting contests in earlier times and is still the venue for an equestrian parade during the city's annual festivities in June.

At the centre of the square is an obelisk commemorating those citizens of Ciutadella who were killed or abducted into slavery during the Turkish raid of 1558. Much of Ciutadella was destroyed, including the *alcázar* or governor's palace. The crenellated town hall, with its

Plaça des Born – sit down, order a coffee and watch the world go by

Opposite: the houses of Maó seem to grow out of the harbour walls

22

Moorish-looking row of palms standing guard, was built in the 19th century on the same site. Peep inside to see the panelled ceilings, portraits of local worthies and the Gothic chamber on the first floor.

Across the square are two 19th-century palaces, those of the Torre-Saura and Salord families, built symmetrically to either side of Carrer Major del Born. Their neo-classical façades are dominated by Italianate loggias; the ground floors facing the square are given over to gift shops and cafés. Near by is the 19th-century theatre, and the adjoining coffee-house, Cercle Artistic, with harbour views.

7
Port de Maó (Maó Harbour)

The glory of Maó – a deep, natural harbour which has protected the Menorcan capital throughout its history.

When the European powers fought over Menorca in the 18th century, the greatest prize was the harbour at Maó. The world's second largest natural harbour, 5km long and up to 900m wide, was wrongly believed to provide an impregnable Mediterranean base.

The best way to see the harbour is on one of the boat tours that leave from Maó and Es Castell in summer. The water is deep but it remains incredibly clear and from a glass-bottomed boat you can see the sea bed.

From the water you get the best views of the 18th-century houses lining either side. High on a cliff between Maó and Es Castell is the Hotel del Almirante, a plumred Georgian villa which was the home of the British Admiral Collingwood, Lord Nelson's second in command. Facing it on the north shore is Sant Antoni (Golden Farm), where Nelson is said to have stayed in 1799.

Between Maó and the harbour entrance are three islands. The first, Illa del Rei (King's Island), was the first place to be 'liberated' by Alfonso III; when the British built a hospital here, it was known as 'Bloody Island'. Next comes Illa Plana (Flat Island), a former quarantine island; this function was taken over in 1900 by the largest island, Lazareto, whose high walls were designed to prevent infections from reaching Maó. South of Lazareto, at the entrance to the harbour, are the ruins of Fort Sant Felip; to the north is the headland of La Mola, the most easterly point in Spain.

✠ 29F2

🍴 Waterfront restaurants at Maó & Es Castell (££–£££)

🚌 Buses between Maó & Es Castell

🚢 Boat tours of the harbour from Maó & Es Castell in summer

↔ Maó (► 30), Es Castell (► 70), Fort Sant Felip (► 76)

8
S'Albufera des Grau

🕀 29E3

🕐 Free access to national park

🍴 At Es Grau (£)

🚌 Buses from Maó to Es Grau in summer

↔ Shangri-La (► 85)

A protected wetland area close to the east coast which acts as an important refuge for aquatic birds.

There used to be many more areas of wetland around the Menorcan coast, but most were drained for agriculture by the British or reclaimed for tourist *urbanizacións* in the 1960s. Of those that survive, S'Albufera is the largest and most important. A 70-hectare lagoon is separated from the sea by a barrier of sand, creating salt-water marshes beside a freshwater lake.

The shores of the lake make a peaceful place to stroll, but the main appeal is definitely for bird-watchers. In winter there are migrant colonies of osprey and booted eagles; in spring and autumn the lake attracts numerous waders and wildfowl. Species regularly seen here include cormorants, herons, spoonbills and terns. In summer you also have to be prepared for mosquitoes.

The lake is separated from the beach at Es Grau by pine woods and dunes. Es Grau is an old-fashioned seaside village, with fishing boats in the harbour and white houses down to the water's edge. The large beach is perfect for children as the water is shallow all the way out to Illa d'en Colom, seen across a channel 400m out to sea.

In summer you can take boat trips to the island, where there is a choice of sunny or shady beaches. This is the largest of Menorca's offshore islands; there is evidence of early habitation, with Roman ruins and a Byzantine church. The island, home to a protected species of lizard, is now part of the S'Albufera National Park.

S'Albufera is at the centre of the Unesco Biosphere Reserve on Menorca

9
Son Bou

A long stretch of fine sandy beach with marshes, caves and an early Christian church.

Much of the south coast is made up of small, indented coves; Son Bou could hardly be more different. The longest beach on Menorca, it has almost 3km of pale golden sand, a sunbather's dream with facilities from beach bars to water-skiing and windsurfing. The water shelves gently and swimming is generally safe, but there are occasional dangerous currents so you should look out for the red and green flags. The beach is so long that it rarely gets crowded; it is always possible, especially at the western end, to find your own secluded spot.

✚ 29D2

🍴 Bars & restaurants (£–££)

🚌 Buses from Maó to Son Bou & Club San Jaime in summer, plus a shuttle 'train' connecting the hotels to the beach

↔ Torre d'en Gaumés (► 26)

At the east end of the beach, beneath two ugly hotels, is one of Menorca's more remarkable ancient monuments – a 5th-century Christian basilica, discovered in 1953. Similar to North African churches of the same period, it has three naves divided by pillars and a huge font, carved from a single stone. When you realise how long it lay hidden beneath the sand you wonder what further treasures are still waiting to be uncovered.

In the cliffs above the basilica are some large prehistoric burial caves, used as summer houses by Menorcan families. Climb up to these caves for the best views over the beach. Above the west end of the beach, separated by marshland, is the purpose-built resort of Sant Jaume Mediterrani. This has everything you could want for a family holiday – pools, shops, discos, plus the popular Club San Jaime with its water-chutes and labyrinthine maze.

Son Bou – a perfect beach for families

25

10
Torre d'en Gaumés

29D2

Free access

None

Son Bou (► 25)

An atmospheric abandoned village with impressive Bronze Age monuments and views over the south coast.

The extensive prehistoric settlement of Torre d'en Gaumés contains several well-preserved Talaiotic buildings. Most of it dates from around 1400 BC, though there is an even older sepulchre near by and evidence of habitation until Roman and perhaps medieval times.

Get there by following the signs from the Alaior-Son Bou road. As soon as you leave this road, the three *talaiots* are visible in the distance, 2km away down a country lane. A paved road leads around the site, making this the one prehistoric site in Menorca which is accessible to wheelchairs and pushchairs, though even then you do not have access to some of the more interesting areas.

Besides the three *talaiots*, there is a *taula* whose horizontal stone has collapsed, enabling you to appreciate its design, with a carefully hollowed-out centre to fit on top of the vertical stone. (It is possible that the hollow was enlarged at a later date for use as a Roman sarcophagus.) Near by is the best-preserved example of a hypostyle chamber, a roofed building with columns, possibly used as a dwelling but more likely as a sheep shelter or grain store. There is also an ingenious water storage and filtration system, probably Roman, with channels dug into the rock beneath a large flat surface.

This is a peaceful spot, with wild flowers growing among the ruins and views stretching from Monte Toro (► 20) to the south coast.

A glimpse of an ancient culture – the remains of the prehistoric village of Torre d'en Gaumés

What To See

MENORCA

Cap de Cavalleria

itja

Cala Tirant
Cala Tirant
Fornells
Platges de Fornells
Port de Fornells
Ses Salines

Na Guillemassa
Punta Pantiné
Cala Pudent
Son Parc
Punta Codolar
Arenal d'en Castell
Na Macaret
Port d'Addaia
En Brut
Cap de Favàritx

mego

ercadal
Sa Roca
358m
Monte Toro
172m
Puig de S'Albaida
Cala Presili
Cala Morella Nou
Cala de Sa Torreta
Sa Torreta
Illa d'en Colom
S'Albufera des Grau
Es Grau
Punta de Sa Galera
112m
Puig Menor
Shangri-La

striches Menorca
Alaior
CAMÍ D'EN KANE

Jaume errani
Bou
Torre d'en Gaumés
Torralba d'en Salord
Rafal Rubí Nou
MAÓ (MAHÓN)
Cala Mesquida
Sant Antoni
Cap Negre
Torre Llisà Vell
Talatí de Dalt
Port de Maó
Cala Llonga
Basifica
Algendar
La Mola
So Na Caçana
Es Castell
Torelló
Cala En Porter
Sant Climent
Llucmaçanes
Trepucó
Fort Sant Felip
Cova d'en Xoroi
Son Vitamina
Hipódromo
Cala de Sant Esteve
Cales Coves
Aeroport de Menorca
Molí de Dalt
Trebalúger
Fort de Marlborough
Es Canutells
S'Ullastrar
Sant Lluís
Cala Canutells
Torret
S'Algar
Binidalí
Binissafúller
Cala Torret
Cala d'Alcaufar
Cap d'en Font
Binibeca Vell
Punta Prima
Punta Prima
Biniancolla
Illa de l'Aire

D   E   F

Maó

You cannot separate Maó from its harbour – without it, the city would not be there. The harbour is the reason why the great powers fought over Menorca for so long; it is the reason why the British moved the capital to Maó in 1722.

The best way to arrive in Maó is by boat, sailing into the harbour past its various islands and watching as the city appears, 25m up on the cliff face, a jumble of attractive white-washed houses which seem to grow out of the old sea walls. Ferries from Barcelona, cruise ships and naval vessels, luxury yachts and even the odd fishing boat share space in the deep, clear waters and the narrow waterfront road is lined with restaurants and bars. Come here on a summer evening, when the buzz of conversation is echoed by the water, and you will understand how Maó is still, more than anything else, a city by the sea.

---

*'June, July, August
and Maó
are the best ports in the
Mediterranean.'*

ANDREA DORIA
Genoese admiral (1468–1560)

Maó

There was a city here in Roman times; its name, Magón, may be that of Hannibal's brother but is more likely derived from a Phoenician word meaning 'shelter'. Modern Maó dates from the Catalan conquest; it was Alfonso III, the conqueror, who began both the Church of Santa Maria and the city walls, of which only the gateway of Port de Sant Roc survives.

Alfonso III, the founder of modern Maó: his statue stands in Plaça Conquesta

The greatest influence on the city you see today, though, is probably British. It was the British who moved the capital to Maó and filled it with Georgian-style architecture not seen anywhere else in Spain. Streets such as Carrer Isabel II are adorned with grand 18th-century houses, with furniture in the style of Sheraton and Chippendale and bow-windows (*boinders* in local language) leaning across the pavement.

For three centuries Maó (which is frequently still referred to by its Spanish name, Mahón) has had to serve its foreign rulers, whether British, French or Spanish. The result is a city that is serious rather than stylish, industrious rather than flamboyant. At times its status as a capital makes it feel like a much bigger city; at other times, when work is done for the day and everyone greets everyone else by name during the evening *passeig* across the Plaça de S'Esplanada, it feels like little more than a small village.

31

What to See in Maó

AJUNTAMENT (TOWN HALL) ✪

🚹 34B2
✉ Plaça Constitució
☎ 36 98 00
🕐 During office hours
🍴 Near by in Plaça Bastió
(£–££)
✋ Free
↔ Santa Maria (➤ 37)

Mao's town hall was built in 1613 but completely refash-ioned in 1788 with the addition of an English clock, a gift from the first British governor Sir Richard Kane. You can visit the building during office hours. A stone stairway leads to the entrance hall, containing the British coat of arms, removed from Fort Sant Felip (➤ 76) in 1887 and taken to Palma de Mallorca, from where it was returned to Maó in 1971. The next room is lined with portraits of former governors, including the Count of Lannion (the first French governor) and the Count of Cifuentes, the first Spanish governor following British rule. Also in this room is a barely legible stone tablet dating from the 1st century and declaring 'Magón' to be a Roman city. Near here is the municipal debating chamber, with velvet armchairs for the deputies and wooden benches for the public.

The town hall contains the records of a city going back almost 2,000 years

ATENEU ✪

🚹 34A2
✉ Carrer de Cifuentes 25
☎ 36 05 53
🕐 Mon–Sat 10–1, 4–9
🍴 In Plaça de S'Esplanada
(£–££)
✋ Free
↔ Plaça de S'Esplanada
(➤ 36)

For a city with the population of a small provincial town, Maó has a rich intellectual tradition, perhaps a result of the exposure to so many foreign cultures and ideas. The real focus of Mao's intellectual life is this scientific, literary and artistic association, founded in 1905. Visitors are welcome to see the collections of maps, ceramics, watercolours and fossils. This is a museum like museums used to be, kept open by devoted scholars.

CALA FIGUERA ⭐⭐

Take the long stairway which leads from the city centre down to the waterfront, turn right by the ferry station along the Moll de Llevant, and after about half an hour, as the road bends to the right, you enter the deep cove of Cala Figuera. This is the fashionable area of Maó – the *club marítimo* is here, the city's best hotel is up on the cliff and there are restaurants ranging from fresh fish to pizza and up-market *nouvelle cuisine*. Sitting in the lunchtime sun, you have a perfect view of the Illa del Rei in the middle of Maó harbour. Once known as 'the English creek' because English boats would moor here for fresh water, it is now – controversially – the storage site for Menorca's petrol reserves. There is a long-standing plan to move the tanks across the harbour to the naval base to create more space at Cala Figuera for a marina and avoid the need for petrol tankers to disfigure the lunchtime scene on the waterfront.

COLLECCIÓ HERNÁNDEZ MORA ⭐

Hernández Mora (1902–84) was a local historian, author and teacher who devoted much of his spare time to collecting historic documents and artefacts in order to preserve his beloved Menorcan heritage. When he died childless, he left his collection to the city of Maó and it has been turned into this small museum in the cloisters of the Església del Carme (➤ 34). The chief part of the display comprises furniture and books; there is also a fascinating collection of maps.

🚩 34C2
🍴 Lots of restaurants (££-£££)
↔ Port de Maó (➤ 23), Es Castell (➤ 70)

Above: *by the harbour at Cala Figuera – the place to see and be seen*

🚩 34C2
✉ Entrance on Plaça Miranda
☎ 35 05 97
🕐 Mon–Fri 10–1
🍴 Near by (£-££)
💷 Cheap
↔ Església del Carme (➤ 34)

MAÓ

Port de Maó

ESGLÉSIA DEL CARME ⭘⭘

- 34C2
- Plaça de Carme
- 36 24 02
- Near by (£–££)
- Free
- Collecció Hernández Mora (➤ 33)

This massive baroque church was built in 1751 as a Carmelite convent but extensive damage during the Spanish Civil War means that most of what you see is heavily restored. The stern façade leads to a bright interior with bare stone walls and arches and a vaulted ceiling. During the original building of the church, a Roman necropolis was discovered in the vaults, along with various coins and urns which are now in the Museu de Menorca (➤ 36). Next door to the church, in the cloisters of the old convent, fruit and vegetables are sold beneath the whitewashed arches with angelic gargoyles looking on in what must be one of the most unusual settings anywhere for a covered market. This is a good place to buy Mahón cheese, as well as cured hams and local sausages.

The bare stone walls of Església del Carme were designed to make it harder to attack

A Walk Around Maó

Begin in Plaça de S'Esplanada (► 36) with your back to the barracks and take Carrer Ses Moreres in the right-hand corner. Head down this street, noting the bust of Dr Orfila (► 14) outside No 13.

Continue into another shopping street, Carrer Hannóver, which drops sharply to Plaça Constitució. Turn right into Carrer Nou; this brings you to Plaça Reial. Turn left to reach Plaça del Carme. Cross this square diagonally to look into the cloistered market then head down the steps to the fish market in Plaça d'Espanya.

You could drop down to the waterfront here – but to continue your city walk, follow the stone railings around the square into Plaça Conquesta, with its statue of the Conqueror, Alfonso III. The narrow alley off the square to the right gives a splendid view of the harbour.

Leave Plaça Conquesta diagonally opposite where you entered to return to Plaça Constitució. Turn right by the town hall then bear left into Carrer Isabel II, whose Georgian houses back on to the harbour walls.

The road ends at the Museu de Menorca (► 36).

Turn left to enter a maze of narrow streets and whitewashed houses. Another left turn, then right, brings you to Carrer Sant Antoni, emerging beside an old convent, now an art gallery. Turn left to reach Pont de Sant Roc, the only remaining section of the city walls. Turn right into Plaça Bastió and cross this square to enter Carrer d'Alaior. Turn right at the end to return to Plaça de S'Esplanada.

Distance
3km

Time
1 hour

Start/end point
Plaça de S'Esplanada
🚩 34A1
🚌 Buses from all over the island terminate here

Lunch
Sa Parada (£)
✉ Plaça de S'Esplanada 64
☎ 36 52 13

Plaça de S'Esplanada, where the walk begins and ends, is the best place to see the people of Maó at play

34A3
⊠ Plaça des Monestir
☎ 35 09 55
🕐 Apr–Oct: Tue–Fri
10:30–1:30, 6–9; Sat–Sun
10–2. Nov–Mar: Tue–Sat
10–1, 5:30–8; Sat–Sun
10–2
🍴 Near by in Plaça Bastió
(£–££)
💷 Cheap

Opposite: Santa Maria is the closest thing Maó has to a cathedral

34A1
🍴 Lots of restaurants &
cafés (£–££)
🚌 Buses to Maó from
across the island
terminate here
↔ Ateneu (► 32)
❓ Market Tue, Sat

Menorca's largest museum is housed in the cloisters of a former monastery

MUSEU DE MENORCA ✪✪

Come here after exploring Menorca's archaeological sites to discover what happened to all the finds and to piece together the missing links in your knowledge of prehistoric Menorca.

Coins, pottery and funerary objects from several different cultures are gathered under one roof, together with the island's largest collection of fine arts. The setting, in the cloisters of the old Franciscan monastery, is delightful – a light, airy courtyard with an old well at its centre leads on to a series of temporary exhibition rooms, with the main museum upstairs.

The most interesting feature of the attached Church of Sant Francesc is the octagonal Chapel of the Immaculate Conception, a florid confection of roses and vines in brilliant white Churrigueresque (Spanish baroque) style.

PLAÇA DE S'ESPLANADA ✪✪

This esplanade – the square between the barracks and the streets of the old town – is the best place to go to see the people of Maó at play. There are pigeons and palm trees, fountains and flower beds, a bowling alley and a children's playground which is busy from late afternoon until dusk. Old men sit in the shade reading newspapers; teenagers queue for popcorn and ice-cream.

On Tuesdays and Saturdays there is an open-air clothes market here; on Sundays, street entertainers join the crowds. During Maó's festivals Plaça de S'Esplanada acts as an outdoor venue for concerts and parties. The square is lined with cafés – a good place to come during the evening *passeig* to sit with a drink, feeling the pulse of Maó.

PORT DE MAÓ (MAÓ HARBOUR ► 23, TOP TEN)

SANTA MARIA ✪✪

Maó's main church was begun soon after the Catalan conquest, then rebuilt in neo-classical style in the 18th century in a gesture of defiance to the island's British, Protestant rulers. Everything here is done on a massive scale. A huge, forbidding façade, like a great ochre cliff-face broken only by the incongruous presence of four sash windows, leads through the entrance portal to a long, single nave. Most people come here to see (or hear) the organ, built by the Swiss maker Johann Kyburz and imported from Barcelona during the Napoleonic Wars with the help of the British. During the summer there are daily concerts of organ music.

- ⊞ 34B2
- ✉ Plaça Constitució
- ☎ 36 39 49
- 🍴 Near by in Plaça Bastió (£–££)
- 🎵 Free (organ concerts – cheap)
- 🔄 Ajuntament (► 32)
- ❓ Organ concerts, Jul–Sep, Mon–Sat 11AM

TEATRE PRINCIPAL ✪

When the Greek community was forced out of Maó in the late 18th century, the former Orthodox church was converted into a dance hall; when that outgrew its usefulness, this theatre was built instead. Designed by a Florentine architect in 1829 and full of Italianate touches, it was comprehensively restored in 1997. Nowadays it is mostly used as a cinema but plays are still staged and it is also the venue for Maó's spring opera season.

- ⊞ 34B1
- ✉ Costa d'en Deià 46
- 🍴 In Plaça Reial (£)
- ❓ Opera season, Mar–Apr (contact Ajuntament, ☎ 36 98 00)

XORIGUER ✪

Menorca's leading gin distillery promotes itself as a tourist attraction in order to entice customers in. In practice all you get to see is the shop, with a few copper stills bubbling away behind glass. The good news, though, is that you can drink as much as you like – not just gin, but herbal liqueurs ranging from camomile to carob. Another speciality is *calent*, made with aniseed, cinnamon and saffron and served warm to clients 'on the house' by bar owners in Ciutadella each Christmas.

- ⊞ 34B3
- ✉ Moll de Ponent 93
- ☎ 36 21 97
- 🕐 Summer: 8–7 Mon–Fri & Sat morning. Closed Sun. Winter: Mon–Fri 1-7
- 🍴 On the waterfront (££–£££)
- 🎵 Free
- 🔄 Port de Maó (► 23)

Ciutadella

Where Maó is bureaucratic, Ciutadella is artistic; where Maó has power, Ciutadella has style. The nobility and the church stayed behind when the capital was moved to Maó with the result that Ciutadella remains a pure Catalan city, undiluted by British or French architecture or the ideas that colonial rulers brought in their wake.

There were Carthaginian and Roman settlements here, and the Arabs made it their capital, but Ciutadella, Menorca's second town, reached its zenith in the 17th century when the island's richest families settled here.

Wander the maze of narrow streets fanning out from the cathedral, their Gothic palaces each marked by a coat of arms carved above the door; sit beneath the palm trees in the Plaça des Born at dusk; join the citizens of Ciutadella for their annual festival, when richly caparisoned horses prance through the streets, and you begin to appreciate the truth of the Count of Cifuentes' *bon mot*.

'Maó may have more people, but Ciutadella has more souls.'

COUNT OF CIFUENTES
Governor of Menorca (1782)

What to See in Ciutadella

CASTELL SANT NICOLAU ★

This 17th-century octagonal defence tower, with drawbridge, moat and turrets, stands alone on a limestone platform halfway around the Passeig Marítim (➤ 42). Nowadays it is used as an exhibition centre, with displays on environmental themes and occasional art exhibitions. The real reason for coming here, though, is to watch the sun set over the sea and see the mountains of Mallorca appear, silhouetted against a pink sky. It is beautiful and romantic, but you won't be alone.

✚ 28A4
✉ Passeig Marítim
◷ Mon–Sat 7:30–9:30PM in summer; Sat only in winter
🍽 None
🖐 Free
↔ Passeig Marítim (➤ 42)

CATEDRAL ★★

Ciutadella has been Menorca's religious capital since Arab times; when Alfonso III conquered the island in 1287, one of his first acts was to have the main mosque reconsecrated as a church. The Catalan-Gothic structure took shape over the next 75 years, though part of the old mosque still remains in the ramp of the north tower, reminiscent of an Islamic minaret. The church finally gained its cathedral status in 1795, when a bishopric was restored to Ciutadella after an absence of 1,300 years.

Outside, a stark, windowless wall – probably added after the Turkish raid on Ciutadella in 1558 – leads to thick square buttresses. Inside, an aisleless nave leads to a pentagonal apse and a dozen side chapels. Most of the interior fittings were destroyed during the Spanish Civil War and what you see is heavily restored – a plaque in the floor pays tribute to Bishop Pascual Marroig, who restored the cathedral between 1939 and 1967.

✚ 28A4
✉ Plaça de la Catedral
☎ 38 07 39
◷ 9–1, 6–9 daily
🍽 Near by (£–££)
🖐 Free
↔ Plaça des Born (➤ 22), Museu Diocesà (➤ 40), Museu del Pintor Torrent (➤ 41), Palau Salord (➤ 42), Ses Voltes (➤ 44)

Ciutadella's harbour is lined with fashionable fish restaurants, where the fish comes straight off the boat

+ 28A4
✉ Camí de Maó 1
🕐 Tue, Thu, Sat 10–1, 4–7
🍴 Bar Es Molí downstairs; restaurants (£–££) in Plaça Alfons III
🎟 Free

MOLÍ DES COMTE ✪

First built in 1778 for the Count of Torre-Saura, this windmill fell into disrepair until it was restored in the 1960s by the present Count; it was opened to the public in 1994. A winding 73 steps lead to the tower, from where there is a splendid view of the city's rooftops through the sails, but other than this there is little to detain all but the most dedicated windmill enthusiast. Just as diverting is the bar downstairs, with pool tables and video games in the vaults of the old mill.

+ 28A4
✉ Carrer Seminari
☎ 38 04 45
🕐 Tue–Sun 10–1:30 in summer; Sat 11–1 in winter
🍴 Near by (£–££)
🎟 Cheap
↔ Catedral (► 39), Ses Voltes (► 44)

MUSEU DIOCESÀ ✪

The Museum of the Diocese of Menorca is housed in a former Augustine monastery close to the cathedral. Peaceful baroque cloisters lead on to a series of rooms containing ecclesiastical treasures including vestments, chalices and reliquaries. There is also a room devoted to a collection of prehistoric finds, though these are not as interesting as those in the Museu Municipal (► 41).

Behind the museum, in Plaça de la Libertat, is the city's lively food market, with stalls selling fresh fruit, vegetables, meat, cheese and fish.

> ### Did you know ?
>
> *The palm-lined Plaça Alfons III, opposite the windmill, was formerly the gateway to Ciutadella – and the pedestrian street beyond, which begins as Carrer de Maó and leads to Plaça des Born, was the city's main thoroughfare. The gateway was demolished in 1868 when the city walls were torn down to create what is now the ring road Sa Contramurada.*

Above: *the tower of the Diocesan Museum*

Opposite: *3,000 years of Menorcan history can be traced at the Municipal Museum*

MUSEU MUNICIPAL ✪✪

The Bastió de Sa Font was built as a fortress in the late 17th century; it was subsequently used as a grain store, a gas factory and a water tank before being fully renovated and opened as the city's museum in 1995. The displays, neatly laid out in a long, bright, vaulted gallery, are carefully captioned and there are leaflets available in English to help you to find your way around.

The museum tells the history of Menorca from pre-Talaiotic to Muslim times through a collection of fascinating exhibits gathered from archaeological excavations around the island – bone knives which go back 3,000 years, ancient spears and slingshots, Roman coins, jewellery, oil-lamps and dice. The most gruesome display case contains a collection of Iron Age skulls, which show that the Talaiotic culture had developed advanced techniques in cranial pathology. As well as head wounds caused by blows from weapons, there are fractures which are the result of trepanning, or surgery. Signs of scarring show that the patient survived the operation and made a full recovery.

✚ 28A4
✉ Bastió de Sa Font
🕐 Mon–Sat 10–1, 7–9 in summer; Sat 10–1 in winter
🍴 In city centre (£–££)
👋 Cheap
↔ Santa Clara (➤ 44)

MUSEU ✪
DEL PINTOR TORRENT

José Torrent, a native of Ciutadella who was born in 1904, is widely considered one of the two greatest Menorcan painters of the 20th century – the other is Joan Vives Llull, from Maó. After his death in 1990, a number of Torrent's works were gathered together in an old town house close to the Plaça des Born. You can follow his development from youthful Impressionism to the Expressionism of his final years, and see for yourself why he is known as 'the Van Gogh of Menorca'.

✚ 28A4
✉ Carrer Sant Rafel 11
🕐 11–1, 7:30–9:30 daily in summer; Fri–Sat 7–9pm and Sat 11–1 in winter
🍴 Near by (£–££)
👋 Free
↔ Plaça des Born (➤ 22), Catedral (➤ 39), Palau Salord (➤ 42)

PALAU SALORD ✪✪

The streets of the old city are filled with 17th–century palaces, built by Menorca's aristocratic families when they moved to Ciutadella from their country estates. Most are still owned by the original families, in some cases the descendants of those who were rewarded in 1287 when Alfonso 'the Liberal' divided up his new conquest among his followers and friends.

Peep into any of these palaces when the doors are open and you see fine courtyards with stone stairways, Italianate loggias and galleried arcades. Most, including the Torre-Saura palace on Plaça des Born and the Martorell palace on Carrer de Santíssim, are closed to the public; for a glimpse of aristocratic living you have to visit the Palau Salord on the Plaça des Born. Among the riches on display are antique furniture, tapestries and oil paintings, gilded mirrors and a frescoed ballroom.

Palau Salord is typical of the noble mansions which dominate the old town of Ciutadella

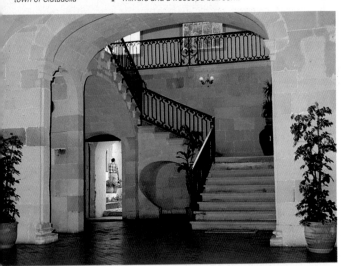

PASSEIG MARÍTIM ✪✪

This wide promenade, completed in 1997, follows the seafront around the peninsula from the small beach at Cala des Degollador to the marina. This is the place to come at dusk to watch the sun set over the sea and join the locals on their evening *passeig*. Mothers and grandmothers, teenagers holding hands – the whole population of Ciutadella seems to be there. As the promenade approaches the city centre, a flight of steps leads down to the port where you can walk around the harbour and look up above the old city walls to the Plaça des Born.

PLAÇA DES BORN (➤ 22, TOP TEN)

A Walk Around Ciutadella

Begin in Plaça des Born (➤ 22) with your back to the town hall.

Go up Carrer Major del Born, directly facing the obelisk. Turn left in front of the cathedral along Carrer Ca'l Bisbe.

This takes you past the bishop's palace to Palau Squella, a fine 18th-century mansion.

Turn left at the end of the street, then right into Carrer Sant Rafel, passing the Museu del Pintor Torrent (➤ 41) and continuing into Carrer Sant Miquel. At the first crossroads, a narrow passage on the left leads to the old sea walls.

Look down on to Pla de Sant Joan, a large open space which is the venue for the city's main festival in June (➤ 116).

Turn right to reach the old fort, now the Museu Municipal (➤ 41), then turn right on to Carrer Portal de Sa Font. Passing the convent of Santa Clara (➤ 44), continue along the narrow street ahead then turn left into Carrer Sant Antoni to reach Plaça Nova.

Ahead, Carrer de Maó leads to Plaça Alfons III, a popular meeting-place and a good lunch stop.

Turn right along the ring road, then right again into Carrer Alaior. When you reach the market turn right, then left into Carrer del Socors and left again into Carrer Seminari, an elegant shopping street. At the end of this street turn right then right again into Carrer del Roser. When you reach the cathedral, turn left to return to Plaça des Born.

This walk can be combined with a pleasant stroll along the Passeig Marítim (➤ facing page). Go in the evening and you will be among the locals doing their *passeig*. Leave Plaça des Born on its southwest side (Plaça de S'Esplanada), then join the seafront promenade and follow it to its end. Return to Plaça de S'Esplanada along Carrer de Mallorca (a walk of about 30 minutes).

Distance
2km

Time
1 hour

Start/end point
Plaça des Born
⊞ 28A4

Lunch
Ca's Quinto (££)
✉ Plaça Alfons III 3
☎ 38 10 02

The back streets of Ciutadella seem designed for strolling

🕀 28A4
✉ Carrer Portal de Sa Font
☎ 38 27 78
🕐 Mon–Fri 8–2, 4:30–8; Sat 4:30–8
🍴 Near by (£–££)
♿ Free
↔ Museu Municipal (➤ 41)

Detail from the convent of Santa Clara

🕀 28A4
🍴 Lots of restaurants & bars (£–££)
↔ Catedral (➤ 39), Museu Diocesà (➤ 40)

SANTA CLARA ✪

Founded by Alfonso III immediately after the Reconquest in 1287, this convent was destroyed during the Turkish attack on Ciutadella in 1558 and rebuilt 56 years later. It was destroyed again during the Spanish Civil War and the building you see today dates from 1945. It is still a working convent and only the church is open to visitors; it is plainly decorated with white stone arches and the kaleidoscopic altar-piece, with its dazzling rainbows and purple skies, comes as quite a shock.

SES VOLTES ✪✪

This pedestrian alley at the heart of the old city, also named after the local historian José-Maria Quadrado, is the focal point of Ciutadella's social life. This is where café life reigns, as people spend their *siesta* sitting on canvas chairs in the shade of Moorish-style arches, then return during the evening *passeig* for a drink outside one of the bars on Plaça Nova before checking out the row of billboards to see what is on at the cinema.

Did you know ?

Santa Clara was at the centre of a diplomatic incident in 1749 when three young women fled the convent and placed themselves under the protection of their British boyfriends, who were soldiers in the nearby garrison. The British governor, General Blakeney, refused to hand them back, but to satisfy the church authorities he had the room in which they were staying sealed by a priest each night. Eventually the three sets of lovers were allowed to marry. One of the neighbouring streets is still called Que No Passa – nobody shall pass.

A Drive From Ciutadella to Maó

The map of Menorca is dominated by one road, the C721 connecting Maó to Ciutadella. A drive along the length of this road passes three inland towns and several prehistoric sites.

Start on the edge of Ciutadella, at the round-about with the sculpture of a prancing horse.

Pass the football stadium and the industrial estate on your left, with factory shops competing for your attention. After 4km the car park for Naveta des Tudons (➤ 21) is reached on the right; shortly after this there are more turn-offs to Torre Trencada (➤ 90) and Torre Llafuda (➤ 89). After 9km, skirt a crest by Castillo Menorca where you will have your first view of the central mountains.

After passing the manor house of Binisues (➤ 52) on your left, a series of bends takes you up to Ferreries (➤ 74). The road continues to Es Mercadal (➤ 72), with Monte Toro (➤ 20) dominating the view.

Shortly after bypassing Es Mercadal, Camí d'en Kane (➤ 87) leads off to the left; next you climb a twisting hill to a picnic area overlooking the rock formation known as Sa Penya de S'Indio, because of its apparent resemblance to an Indian brave. From here the road bypasses Alaior (➤ 48), then goes fast and straight to Maó.

Turn right after the industrial estate, following signs for 'Centre Ciutat'. Turn left at the next roundabout to reach Plaça de S'Esplanada, the start of the walk around Maó (➤ 35).

You can return to Ciutadella the same way, or combine this with one of the other drives (➤ 51 and 87). Alternatively, take the pretty country roads between Es Mercadal and Ferreries via Es Migjorn Gran (➤ 73).

Distance
44km one way

Time
1 hour

Start point
Ciutadella
✚ 28A4

End point
Maó
✚ 29E2

Lunch
Molí des Racó (££)
✉ Carrer Vicario Fuxà 53, Es Mercadal
☎ 37 53 92

Green-shuttered houses in Ferreries, Menorca's highest town

Around the Island

Outside the two cities, Menorca's attractions fall into three main categories, and to get a complete picture of the island you need to visit them all. There are the small inland towns, all of which reward an hour or two's gentle strolling. There are the prehistoric sites, more than a thousand in all, of which the most important are found in an area south and east of Alaior. Finally there is the coast, which is never far away – from huge modern resorts with all facilities to deserted coves where pine-fringed cliffs lean into the sea.

The two halves of Menorca came together 100 million years ago. The north, or *tramuntana*, is all dark soil and slate; its craggy coast, scarred by the north wind, is broken by deep inlets and stony beaches backed by dunes. The south, or *migjorn*, is milder and more sheltered, a low limestone plateau riven with gorges which spill into the sea along beaches of fine sand.

'All its life, its history, its landscape, even the idiosyncrasies of its inhabitants, are closely influenced by the sea.'

REV FERNANDO MARTÍ CAMPS
History of Menorca (1971)

What to See Around the Island

ALAIOR ✪✪

✚ 29D3
🍴 Bars & cafés; The
Cobblers restaurant (££)
🚌 Buses from Maó &
Ciutadella
↔ Torralba d'en Salord
(► 89)
❓ Market Thu; Festa de
Sant Llorenç: Sun
following 10 Aug

Menorca's third largest town, 12km west of Maó, was founded by Jaume II of Mallorca in 1304 when he divided the island into seven regions, each with a central market town. The existence of Roman roads around the town, and the wealth of prehistoric remains near by, suggest that it was a centre of population much earlier.

There are few specific sights in Alaior, but it makes a pleasant place to stroll – a town of gleaming white houses huddled together in narrow streets which lead up to the parish Church of Santa Eulàlia at the town's summit. Jaume II built the first church here; it was later fortified by villagers following the Turkish attacks on Maó and Ciutadella. The present baroque church dates from the 17th century.

Another 17th-century church, Sant Diego, was once a Franciscan convent – its peaceful cloisters have been turned into modern flats, set around a courtyard with an old well at its centre. You can enter the cloisters via a vaulted, whitewashed alley beside the church. The style is said to be based on the Spanish colonial missions in Mexico and California. The courtyard, now known as Sa Lluna, is the setting for concerts and folk-dancing in summer.

Alaior is an important centre for the manufacture of shoes, ice-cream and especially Mahón cheese (► 55). You can buy cheese at the Coinga factory shop, which is signposted as you enter the town from the south. The shop sells the full range from *fresco* (fresh and soft) to *añejo* (matured for two years and as strong as Parmesan), as well as various cheesy souvenirs and jars of cheese in olive oil.

Say cheese – especially if you're in Alaior

ARENAL D'EN CASTELL ✪

This popular holiday centre is the most westerly of the trio of resorts reached by heading north from Alaior. Each of the three has its own distinct character and Arenal (the name means 'sandy place') is the brash one. The setting is superb – a near-circular bay with a long arc of fine sand backing on to dunes and pine-fringed cliffs – but it is rather spoilt by the presence of two enormous modern hotels towering over the beach. There is windsurfing and water-skiing; you can hire pedal boats, motorboats, parasols and sunbeds. The shallow water and the presence of a first-aid post make this a safe beach for children.

✚ 29E4
🍴 Several bars & restaurants (£–££)
🚌 Buses from Maó & Fornells in summer
↔ Na Macaret (➤ 77), Port d'Addaia (➤ 78)

Arenal d'en Castell – lovely beach, shame about the rest

ARENAL DE SON SAURA ✪✪

One of Menorca's prettiest beaches is also one of the hardest to reach – by the time you have opened and shut half a dozen farm gates and surveyed the damage to your hire car's suspension, you will begin to wish you'd walked instead (the coastal path from Cala En Turqueta takes about an hour). To get there by car you have to cross farmland and in summer the farmer levies a toll in order to keep down the numbers. But it is worth the effort – two long stretches of white sand, hidden behind fragrant pine wood and neatly divided by a woody outcrop. There are no beach facilities even in summer, so take a picnic.

✚ 28B3
🍴 None
🚤 Boat trips from Ciutadella & Cala En Bosc in summer
↔ Son Catlar (➤ 86)

49

BARRANC D'ALGENDAR (➤ 16, TOP TEN)

BINIBECA VELL ●●●

🗙 29E1
🍴 Several bars &
restaurants (££)
🚌 Buses from Maó in
summer

You'll either love or hate this place – it is difficult to feel anything in between. To some it is an example of tasteful tourist development, based on architectural beauty and local style; to others it is tacky, artificial and ugly. One of the earliest coastal developments in Menorca, it was designed to resemble a Mediterranean fishing village, with whitewashed houses, orange trees and sun-drenched patios filled with geraniums. A maze of narrow alleys, Moorish archways, boats and sea views, it would be stunning if only it were authentic. The first giveaway is the name – would a real fishing village be called *Poblat de Pescadors* ('Fishing Village')? Then there are the notices for 'reception' and 'public relations', and the signs asking people to be quiet. Look beneath the steeple for the village church and you find an alcove with a crucifix inside – the architect needed a church for the postcards but the temporary 'villagers' have no need of a real one.

A new coat of whitewash for Binibeca Vell (above)

You could easily spend your whole holiday here – there is a supermarket, souvenir shops, restaurants and bars, swimming pools, squash courts, a children's play area and a car hire office in case you should want to see Menorca. The nearest beach is 1km away at Binibeca Nou – here you can hire sunshades, loungers and pedal boats and have lunch at a simple wooden shack which claims to be the only place in Menorca where you can drink with your feet in the sea.

A Drive Around the Southeast

This drive takes in Menorca's only stretch of coast road.

Start in Maó, leaving Plaça de S'Esplanada on the airport road. Turn left at the first roundabout and left again at the next. Follow signs to Sant Lluís. Go straight through Sant Lluís (▶ 83) and over the roundabout towards the coast. After 1km, take the right fork to Punta Prima and after another 1km – when you see a huge satellite mast ahead – fork left, climbing a hill and dropping down to the sea. As you enter Punta Prima (▶ 79), a right turn at the first roundabout (Carrer de Llevant) takes you on to the coast road.

Follow this road for 5km until you see Binibeca Vell on your left. After exploring the village, a left turn at the next roundabout leads down to the sea and an idyllic lunch spot on the beach. When this road runs out, turn inland – go left at the T-junction then swing a wide left at the three-way intersection to return to the coast.

Eventually the road leads inland across a rocky landscape, followed by gentle countryside on its way to Sant Climent (▶ 83).

Turn left through the village on to the Cala En Porter road; after 4km, just beyond the turn-off to Cales Coves, take the country road to Alaior on your right.

You cross a typical landscape of meadows and drystone walls, as well as passing some interesting prehistoric sites.

On reaching Alaior (▶ 48), turn right and return to Maó on the main road.

Distance
48km

Time
2 hours plus lunch

Start/end point
Maó
✚ 29E2

Lunch
Los Bucaneros (££)
✉ Binibeca Nou beach
☎ No telephone

Stop off in Alaior to wander the narrow streets

28C4
Beach bar in summer (£)
Cala Pregonda (➤ 17)

BINIMEL-LÀ ✪

Getting to Binimel-là is an adventure in itself. Head north from Es Mercadal along a series of country roads, then follow a wide dust track signposted to Binimel-là. After about 1½km the track forks left to drop down to the beach, where you can park your car beside a freshwater lake.

The beach, backed by sand dunes, is of red sand and pebbles; the water is deep and the absence of shade means you are exposed to the sun and wind. To escape this, head for the smaller sheltered beaches around the bay, popular with nudists – you can get there by ignoring the left fork mentioned above. The main beach has a temporary bar in summer, from where you can hire windsurfing boards, pedal boats and sun loungers. The best reason for coming to Binimel-là, though, is in order to walk to Cala Pregonda (➤ 17).

28C4
Off the C721
Maó–Ciutadella highway at 31km
37 37 28
Apr–Oct, daily 11–7
Restaurant (££)
Moderate
Ferreries (➤ 74), Santa Agueda (➤ 84)

BINISUES ✪

This stately home on the road to Santa Agueda, just west of Ferreries, has been turned into an exhibition of traditional Menorcan life, customs and furniture. The home of the Salort y Martorell family, it retains its original furnishing and paintings, as well as farm buildings filled with old-fashioned tools. The name of the house, like so many in Menorca, reveals the island's Moorish past – *bini* is Arabic for 'sons of'. The restaurant here specialises in traditional Menorcan country cooking.

The furniture at Binisues shows how wealthy Menorcan families used to live

CALA BLANCA ⭐

This pretty pine-fringed cove, just 4km south of Ciutadella, has been blighted in recent years by excessive development. Once there was just a small beach nestling between low limestone cliffs; now it has been engulfed to such an extent that the beach is a mere speck on the map of the 'village'. The beach is overlooked by several restaurants, all competing to attract families with facilities ranging from swimming pools and water slides to games rooms and 'adult entertainment'. At the back of the beach are the remains of a Bronze Age *naveta*.

⊕ 28A3
🍴 Several restaurants & bars (££)
🚌 Buses from Ciutadella in summer
↔ Cala Santandría (▶ 65)

CALA D'ALCAUFAR ⭐⭐

This small creek, 4km southeast of Sant Lluís, is classically Menorcan – fishermen's cottages reach down to the water's edge and the narrow, curving, sheltered inlet is lined with boats and backed by a sandy beach. This was the site of Menorca's first tourist hotel and it is still a popular weekend trip for the people of Sant Lluís. From the beach you can easily climb on to the cliffs, where a short walk leads to a headland crowned by a Martello tower – beneath which are two grottoes that can be entered by boat.

Cala d'Alcaufar was the site of the first British landing on Menorca, in 1708. Just to the north is S'Algar, reached by a separate road or on a recently restored section of the coastal bridleway, Camí de Cavalls. The development here is a lot less restrained and the slopes leading down to the sea are a jumble of villas and apartments.

⊕ 29F1
🍴 Bar/restaurant beside the beach (£)
🚌 Buses from Maó in summer

Above: *Cala d'Alcaufar is one of Menorca's smallest and prettiest resorts*

Food & Drink

Menorca's cookery is rooted in its history. The Arabs introduced almonds, the Spanish brought peppers from America, while the British imported Friesian cattle, still used in today's dairy industry – but the essential ingredients remain truly Mediterranean: garlic, tomatoes and olive oil.

Seafood

Menorca's island cuisine relies heavily on the products of the sea. Most notable – and expensive – are spiny lobsters from Fornells, used in the classic soup *caldereta de langosta* (▶ 98). Fresh prawns and mussels are abundant; other fish includes mullet, sole and sea-bass. Squid is a speciality, stuffed with its own meat; vegetables such as aubergines and peppers are also frequently stuffed with seafood. A true *paella*, from Valencia, consists of saffron rice cooked with meat and fish, but its Menorcan equivalent, *arroz marinera*, is based on seafood. Other rice dishes include *arroz caldoso*, a fish and rice stew.

Mayonnaise
There are numerous legends as to the origins of mayonnaise (*salsa mahonesa*), but the most common has it invented by the Duc de Richelieu's housekeeper during the French occupation of Maó (Mahón). A blend of raw egg, olive oil and a touch of vinegar or lemon juice, it is usually mixed with garlic to make *allioli* and served with fish, rabbit or vegetables.

Meat Dishes

Meat – which could be beef, veal, pork or lamb – is often served roasted with *salsa de grevi* (gravy), a legacy of the British occupation. Menorcans are proud of their various sausages, a by-product of the winter *matança* or slaughter of pigs. The best-known are *sobrasada*, made of minced raw pork with hot peppers, and *botifarró* (blood pudding); others include *carn i xua*, *cuixot* and *salsitxa*. Order a *surtido de fiambres* (plate of cold cuts) and you might get all of these, along with cured ham and Mahón cheese (see opposite).

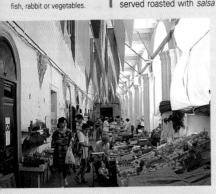

Maó's main market is the best place to buy fresh fruit and vegetables, as well as Mahón cheese

Tapas

Tapas (▶ 94) include octopus, snails and tripe but two of the simplest snacks are *tortilla*, a cold potato omelette, and *pa amb oli*, bread rubbed with tomato, sprinkled with olive oil and topped with ham or cheese. Bakers sell *formatjades* and *empanadillas*, small pies filled with sausage, cheese, tuna or spinach, as well as *bocadillos* (filled rolls).

Café society rules in Ciutadella

Desserts

La Menorquina ice-creams, from Alaior, are sold throughout Spain – as well as ice-creams and sorbets they produce a large range of frozen desserts, from *bikini* to *tarta de whisky*. Sweet biscuits are another local speciality, especially *amargas* and *carquinyols* (almond macaroons), while *ensaimadas* are fluffy, spiral pastries made with lard and dusted with sugar. *Cucusso* is made from honey, raisins and almonds.

Cheese

Cheese has been produced on Menorca since the 14th century and *queso de Mahón* is now one of Spain's leading cheeses, with its own *denominación de origen*. Until recently a seasonal farmhouse cheese, it is now produced industrially from pasteurised milk and exported across the world. Made in square loaves and cured for up to two years, its yellow rind is coated with oil as it matures. Varieties range from *tierno*, eaten mild and young and used to stuff Christmas turkeys, through *semi-curado* and *curado* to the fully mature *añejo*.

Drinks

There is only one wine producer left in Menorca and most wine is imported from mainland Spain. The best reds come from Rioja, made with the *tempranillo* grape and aged in oak. *Cava* is a sparkling wine from Catalunya. Beer is available everywhere – for draught beer, ask for *una caña*. Tap water is safe to drink but everyone drinks mineral water – *agua con gas* is sparkling, *sin gas* is still.

Gin

Gin, a spirit flavoured with juniper berries, was already produced in Menorca before the 18th century but its popularity with British sailors helped to modernise its manufacture. The leading producer is Xoriguer on Maó's waterfront, whose gin is sold in characteristic earthenware bottles called *canecas. Pomada*, gin with lemonade, makes a refreshing *apéritif* – though nowadays you're just as likely to see Menorcans ordering a Scotch on the rocks.

CALA D'ALGAIARENS ✪✪✪

These twin beaches on Menorca's remote northwest coast are reached by crossing the fertile La Vall region until you reach a pair of gateposts surmounted by offputting 'private' signs. In winter you are within your rights to drive on; in summer the landowner levies a toll, justified by the need to restrict traffic pollution in this environmentally sensitive area.

Once through the gates, follow signs to *'playa'* and when the track runs out, walk through the woods – a haven for migrant bee-eaters in spring and summer – to reach the sea. The main beach is a wide horseshoe of golden sand backed by dunes – you can scramble over the low rocks to reach a second beach, Platja d'es Tancats. Both beaches shelve gently into the sea and offer safe bathing in sheltered waters. This is a lovely, peaceful spot which only really gets busy at summer weekends. There are no facilities.

CALA DE SANT ESTEVE ✪✪

St Stephen's Creek is named after an early Christian martyr whose remains were said to have been briefly buried here. A deep, narrow inlet at the mouth of Maó harbour, it is mainly notable for its two military fortifications. On one side are the ruins of Fort Sant Felip (➤ 76); on the other, reached by a tunnel, the seven-sided Marlborough Redoubt, built by the British in the late 18th century to provide extra cover for Fort Sant Felip and believed to be connected to the fort by a subterranean tunnel. Unlike Fort Sant Felip, the redoubt was never destroyed but simply left to rot. It is currently being renovated and will soon be open again for guided tours.

Above: the absence of a beach means that Cala de Sant Esteve has remained peaceful and uncrowded

CALA DEL PILAR ⭐⭐

This is a wild, lonely, beautiful spot which nevertheless gets busy at weekends with locals trying to escape the crowds. Get there by leaving the main Maó to Ciutadella road from the 34km point beneath the Castillo Menorca factory shop; when the tarmac road runs out, you pass through some gates on to farmland and park in a thick grove of oak and pine. Walk for 20 minutes through the woods and you emerge on to reddish dunes; from here you can scramble down to the beach, or over the headland to the next cove. The woods reach almost to the beach and even the dunes are covered in vegetation. This is a conservation area and notices in several languages remind you to keep the beach clean.

🚏 28C4
🍴 Beach bar in summer (£)

A sandy path leads through the woods to Cala del Pilar

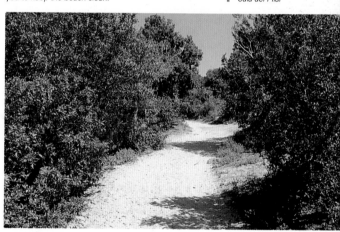

CALA EN BLANES ⭐

The coastline to the west of Ciutadella was once a succession of small beaches and pretty coves; now Cala En Blanes, along with its neighbours Cala En Bruc, Cala En Forcat and Cales Piques, have been swallowed up and merged into one continuous stretch of 'urbanisation'. This is as close as Menorca gets to the mass tourist developments which are so common in Mallorca and the Spanish *costas*, with signs in English and German, villas in fake local style, overcrowding in summer and a complete absence of life in winter. There are good sunset views over Mallorca, and Ciutadella is conveniently close, but otherwise there is little reason to visit these resorts unless you want a little piece of home away from home.

🚏 28A4
🍴 Bars & restaurants (£–££)
🚌 Buses from Ciutadella
↔ Ciutadella (➤ 38)

⊞ 28A3
🍴 Wide choice of restaurants (££)
🚌 Buses from Ciutadella in summer

Above: chic and cheerful – Cala En Bosc

⊞ 29D2
🍴 Bars & restaurants (£–££)
🚌 Buses from Maó in summer

CALA EN BOSC ✪

Just 9km south of Ciutadella and easily reached on a fast road, Cala En Bosc has become one of Menorca's most fashionable resorts. Life revolves around the marina, built on the site of a drained wetland, and lined with trendy restaurants and bars. Small boats can enter the marina through a narrow channel; this is also a departure point for cruises to the remoter coves along the south coast. The neighbouring resort of Son Xoriguer, with its large twin beaches, is a centre for watersports, with schools offering windsurfing, water-skiing, scuba-diving and sailing. Both resorts are heavily developed and not for those seeking peace and quiet.

CALA EN PORTER ✪✪

One of Menorca's earliest beach resorts has grown into a major holiday centre. The setting is lovely – a wide beach leading to a narrow cove where almost unbelievably turquoise water shimmers between tall limestone cliffs. A *barranc*, or ravine, enters the sea via the marshland at the back of the beach. The western side is totally undeveloped, with cliffs tumbling into the sea; the eastern side must once have been the same but the cliffsides are now covered with villas and terrace bars. The most unusual bar is Cova d'en Xoroi, a succession of stairways and rock platforms set in a natural cave high in the cliff-face with dramatic views over the bay and out to sea.

Did you know ?

Xoroi was a legendary Berber pirate who was shipwrecked at Cala En Porter. He abducted a local girl and kept her in his cave for 10 years, during which time she produced four children. When his footprints in the snow gave him away the girl was rescued by her family and Xoroi threw himself into the sea.

CALA EN TURQUETA ✪✪✪

This beautiful spot could easily be destroyed by thoughtless development; as it is it remains blissfully unspoiled. The reason, as with so many of Menorca's beaches, is that it cannot be reached by road. You can get there in a car but only by crossing farmland, with a toll payable in summer – as a result, it never gets too crowded.

Pine-covered cliffs look down on to clear blue water and a beach of soft white sand backs on to extensive pine woods. The beach itself shelves gently into the sea, making it ideal for swimming. For the best views, climb on to the western cliffs – the path here continues to the next cove, Cala des Talaier, and from there to Arenal de Son Saura (➤ 49).

✚ 28B3
🍴 None
🚤 Boat trips from Cala En Bosc & Ciutadella in summer
↔ Ermita de Sant Joan de Missa (➤ 70)

CALA ESCORXADA ✪✪

You used to be able to reach this cove by the coastal footpath from Sant Adeodato (➤ 82) but the path has become a casualty of the ongoing battle between landowners and the authorities over rights of way. By Spanish law, everyone has access to the coast; the problem arises when you need to cross private land to get there. The owner of the land behind Cala Escorxada has denied access to ramblers by erecting barriers. The result is that the cove has become even more remote than it was and all the more attractive for those who do get there – either in a boat or by a long (two hours minimum) and difficult walk from Cala Santa Galdana (➤ 64). Cala Escorxada is typical of the south coast – limestone cliffs, pine woods and a semi-circular beach of soft white sand; it is also good for snorkelling.

✚ 28C3
🍴 None

Head for Cala En Turqueta to escape the crowds – although even here you will not be entirely alone

CALA MACARELLA ✪✪✪

Walk for 30 minutes from the west end of Cala Santa Galdana (➤ 64) across a fragrant headland covered with wild flowers and herbs and you reach this delightful cove where a *barranc* flows into the sea. It's a good way to escape the crowds in high summer but you won't be alone – there is a beach bar which hires out pedal boats, parasols and sunbeds and there is even a rough road to the beach which crosses farmland (a toll is payable in summer) before entering the gorge. Pine trees reach almost to the water's edge, providing welcome shade, and the beach shelves gently into the sea, creating good conditions for swimming. For ease of access combined with unspoilt beauty, this must be one of the best beaches in Menorca.

➕ 28B3
🍴 Cafeteria Susy (£)
🚌 Buses from Ferreries, Maó & Ciutadella to Cala Santa Galdana in summer
↔ Cala Santa Galdana (➤ 64)

Overlooking the bay on its western side are three large caves, once used as burial caves but now in service as holiday homes in summer. If you want more privacy, you can cross the headland above the caves to the even more perfect cove of Cala Macarelleta, where pine-fringed rocks surround a small sandy beach, popular with nudists. From the path on top of the headland you can look down on both coves at once, one of the best views anywhere on Menorca. The more adventurous can get between the two coves by swimming. Cala Macarella and Cala Macarelleta both offer good anchorage for yachts.

The footpath from Cala Santa Galdana to Cala Macarella and Cala Macarelleta (opposite)

CALA MESQUIDA ✪✪

29F2

Es Cap Roig (££)

Despite its proximity to Maó, this remains a peaceful and romantic spot. The capital's citizens come here at weekends, mainly to eat fish in the Cap Roig restaurant, on a slate headland carpeted with wild flowers. At the far end of the village is a wide beach of dark sand protected by cliffs to either side, one of which is dominated by an old watchtower. This was the site of the Duc de Crillon's landing with a Franco-Spanish invasion force in 1781. There is very little modern development (though this was one of Menorca's earliest beach resorts in the 19th century) and the village feels much more remote than it is – and more Menorcan than touristy.

CALA MITJANA ✪✪

28C3

None

Buses from Ferreries, Maó & Ciutadella to Cala Santa Galdana in summer

Cala Santa Galdana (➤ 64)

This beach is best reached on foot from Cala Santa Galdana (➤ 64). The walk starts in Camí de Cavalls above the eastern end of the bay – you can take a car to here or climb up the steps from the beach and turn left. At the end of this short road you go through a gate, bear left and continue through a gap in a wall; from here the way is clearly defined and marked with red dots. The walk takes about 30 minutes, passing the rocky cove of Cala Mitjaneta before arriving at a deep sandy beach surrounded by cliffs riddled with caves. The more adventurous can swim into some of the caves or leap from the cliffs into the cool blue water. Cala Mitjana is popular in summer but numbers are kept down by the need to walk.

Cala Mesquida is Maó's beach, where you see more locals than tourists

CALA MORELL ✪✪

Eight kilometres from Ciutadella on the otherwise deserted northeast coast, Cala Morell is best known for its remarkable collection of prehistoric caves. Dating from the late Bronze and early Iron Ages, and used both as burial caves and as dwellings, they feature circular chambers with central pillars plus windows, chimneys and raised sleeping areas. Some even have elaborately carved motifs on their façades. It is easy to get into most of the caves; if your appetite is whetted, finds from these caves are on display at the Museu de Menorca in Maó (➤ 36) and the Museu Municipal in Ciutadella (➤ 41).

There is a small beach here, reached by steps from the car parks at either end of the village, and there is good swimming and snorkelling from the rock platforms at the foot of the cliffs. The *urbanización* above the beach, a collection of Ibizan-style whitewashed villas, is one of the most exclusive in Menorca. As you wander around the prehistoric caves, you cannot help wondering whether the tourists of 3,000 years' time will be clambering over the ruins of these villas and speculating on late 20th-century life.

Cala Morell
✚ 28B4
🍴 Bars & restaurants (££)
↔ Cala d'Algaiarens (➤ 56)

CALA PREGONDA (➤ 17, TOP TEN)

CALA PRESILI ✪

A short walk from the headland at Cap de Favàritx (➤ 69) brings you to several quiet coves, beginning with Cala Presili. You start the walk by passing through wooden gates between a pair of white pillars 1km from the lighthouse. Cala Presili leads on to Cala Tortuga and then to Cala Morella Nou. All have high grassy dunes, clear white sand and good swimming – and none of them ever gets crowded. Behind the beach at Cala Tortuga is a marshy lake, part of the S'Albufera nature reserve (➤ 24).

✚ 29E3
🍴 None
↔ Cap de Favaritx (➤ 69)

Above: *Cala Morell, where you can play at being a caveman*

63

CALA SANTA GALDANA   ✪✪✪

One of Menorca's most beautiful (and ecologically
important) coves is also one of the most developed – as
such it has become a focus for debate about the extent of
urbanización on the island. Thirty years ago there was not
even a road here; now there are three enormous hotels
and dozens of restaurants and bars.

The 'queen of the coves' takes its name from the Arab
word for the local river; there is in fact no saint Galdana. A
wide arc of golden sand, bounded by wooded cliffs and an
emerald sea, Cala Santa Galdana
enjoys a unique microclimate with
higher temperatures and lower
winds than the surrounding *calas*.
The Barranc d'Algendar (➤ 16)
flows into the sea here, its mouth
widened to form a marina for small
boats. A footbridge across the
stream leads to a rocky outcrop,
almost an island, and a spectacu-
larly sited bar-restaurant where you
dine on a terrace directly
overlooking the sea. For the best
views of the entire bay, follow the
signs to Mirador de Sa Punta on the
eastern cliffs, close to the start of
the walk to Cala Mitjana (➤ 62).
You can also climb up here from the
steps at the eastern end of the
beach.

This is a good place to go in mid-
season as a base for walks along
the gorge or to some of the quieter

beaches in both directions along the coast. In high season it is perfect for family holidays – fun and facilities for the children, safe swimming, and good shady walks for the adults. You can hire windsurfing and snorkelling equipment, pedaloes and motorboats, learn to sail or scuba-dive, or take a boat ride along the coast for a picnic at a peaceful cove.

*Left and below left:
Cala Santa Galdana is
a popular holiday
destination, combining
excellent facilities and
an idyllic setting*

Did you know ?

Cala Santandría was the site of the French landing on Menorca on Easter Sunday 1756. Twelve thousand soldiers, commanded by the Duc de Richelieu, occupied Ciutadella without resistance as the British retreated to Maó. Richelieu sent the British Governor Blakeney a gift of dried fruits; Blakeney responded with six bottles of English beer. A month later Menorca was in French hands.

CALA SANTANDRÍA ✪

This long, narrow creek, just 3km south of Ciutadella, would be pretty if it did not get so crowded. Along with its satellite cove Sa Caleta, it is the beach which Ciutadellans head for at weekends. There are several bars and restaurants, and all the usual facilities, including hire of pedal boats, umbrellas and loungers.

🚩 28A3
🍴 Bars & restaurants (£–££)
🚌 Buses from Ciutadella in summer
🔄 Cala Blanca (➤ 53)

CALA TIRANT ✪

This pair of beaches between Fornells and Cap de Cavallería is reached either by taking the sign to 'Platges de Fornells' just outside Fornells and driving through the Menorca Country Club, or by following the dusty track 2km along the road to Cavallería which leads to the main beach. Both beaches are backed by dunes, marshland and a lake which attracts wading birds. The larger beach has a bar where you can hire umbrellas and sunbeds; there are also facilities for windsurfing and catamaran sailing. Swimming is safe and this is a good beach for children.

🚩 29D4
🍴 Beach bar/restaurant in summer (££)

CALA TREBALÚGER ✪✪

This classic south coast cove, fed by a freshwater stream from a limestone gorge, is one of the hardest to reach. A popular mooring for yachts and pleasure boats in summer, it can only be reached on foot by a walk of about 1½ hours from Cala Santa Galdana (➤ 64) followed by a scramble down to the beach.

🚩 28C3
🍴 None
🚤 Boat trips from Cala En Bosc & Cala Santa Galdana in summer
🔄 Cala Mitjana (➤ 62)

In the Know

If you only have a short time to visit Menorca, or would like to get a real flavour of the island, here are some ideas:

10
Ways To Be A Local

Try to learn a little of the local language, Menorquín as well as Spanish – a simple *bon dia* goes a long way.

Relax, take your time and settle into the Mediterranean way of life.

Take a *siesta* to avoid the afternoon sun – have a long lunch, or rest in the shade.

Do everything late – a late lunch, a late supper, a very late night.

Put on your best clothes and join the evening *passeig*.

Go to the trotting races in Maó and Ciutadella at weekends – and be sure to have a bet.

Find a local *festa* – the best is the Festa de Sant Joan in Ciutadella – and let yourself get swept along by the crowd.

Go topless on the beach if you like but definitely not in restaurants and shops.

Join the locals for a game of bowls in Maó's Plaça de S'Esplanada

Respect the local environment – don't pick wild flowers or leave litter on the beaches.

Adore children – the Menorcans do.

10
Places To Have Lunch By The Sea

Ca'n Delio (££), ✉ Cales Fonts 38, Es Castell ☎ 35 17 11. Grilled sardines by a pretty harbour.

El Mirador (££), ✉ Cala Santa Galdana ☎ 908 799 847. The perfect setting on a terrace overlooking the sea.

Es Cap Roig (££), ✉ Cala Mesquida ☎ 36 37 15. Fresh fish and sea views on a headland north of Maó. Popular with locals.

Es Moll (££), ✉ Moll Commercial, Ciutadella ☎ 48 08 13. Watch the fishermen unload their catch while you eat.

Es Passeig Marítim (££), ✉ Fornells ☎ 37 63 12. Local fish and lobster, or pizzas and home-made desserts.

Es Pla (£££) , ✉ Fornells ☎ 37 66 55. Where the king comes to eat *caldereta de langosta*.

The Menorcans know the value of taking life at a steady pace

Gregal (££), Moll de Llevant 306, Maó ☎ 36 66 06. Modern Mediterranean dishes served beside the harbour at Cala Figuera.

Los Bucaneros (££), ✉ Binibeca Nou (No telephone). Simple fish restaurant in a wooden shack right on the beach. Very romantic. Seasonal only.

Los Toboganes (££), ✉ Cala Blanca ☎ 38 51 68. Mini-golf and a toboggan slope help keep the children amused while you eat.

Susy (£), ✉ Cala Macarella (No tel). Summer bar and restaurant on one of Menorca's most beautiful beaches.

10
Top Activities

- Bird-watching
- Caving
- Diving
- Golf
- Horse-riding
- Sailing
- Swimming
- Walking
- Water-skiing
- Windsurfing

5
Family Beaches

- Arenal d'en Castell
- Cala Blanca
- Cala En Porter
- Cala Santa Galdana
- Son Parc

10
Best Viewpoints

- Cala Macarella/Cala Macarelleta – the headland
- Cap de Cavallería
- Cap de Favàritx
- Castell de Sant Nicolau, Ciutadella (at sunset)
- Cova d'en Xoroi, Cala En Porter
- Mirador de Sa Punta, Cala Santa Galdana
- Monte Toro
- Pont d'es Castell, Maó
- Santa Águeda
- Son Mercer de Baix, Ferreries

5
Quiet Coves

- Cala del Pilar
- Cala En Turqueta
- Cala Escorxada
- Cala Macarelleta
- Cala Pudent (Son Parc)

The trotting races held in Maó and Ciutadella make a popular day out with both locals and tourists

✚ 29D2
🍴 None
🚌 Buses from Maó & Cala
En Porter to Son Vitamina
in summer

CALES COVES ✪✪✪

It takes an effort to get there – a rough four-wheel-drive track or a brisk 30-minute walk through the olive trees from Son Vitamina – but when you arrive at Cales Coves you are greeted by one of the most memorable sights on Menorca. The cliffs looking down on to this sheltered bay are home to more than 100 Bronze Age caves, carved out of the rock and used as both burial chambers and dwellings, with the living and the dead housed side by side. The oldest caves, seen on the left as you arrive, date back to the 9th century BC; follow the footpath over the rocks on your right to reach a second cove, passing more modern caves (4th century BC) whose features include windows, patios and interior cubicles. Some of these have Roman inscriptions, indicating that they continued to be occupied after the Talaiotic period. Some of them, in fact, are still occupied by latter-day troglodytes; you see them collecting water from a spring and bathing nude in the crystal sea. From time to time the authorities try to move these modern cavemen on, but they always return. Peer into some of the uninhabited caves to see hippy paintings of suns, moons and flowers on the walls.

Carvings in the rock face at Cales Coves (top)

The prehistoric villagers chose a good site – the angle of the coves means they are hidden from the open sea. This also provides safe mooring for pleasure boats in summer. The beaches are pebbly rather than sandy, but there is good swimming from the rocks.

CAP DE CAVALLERÍA ✪✪

This headland at Menorca's northernmost point is one of the island's wild places. To get there you have to follow a potholed road across several kilometres of rocky moors, populated by wild goats. On the way you pass the tiny harbour of Sanitja – glancing down at the peaceful scene, just a few boats moored by the water's edge, it is hard to believe that in Roman times the port of Sanisera was Menorca's third city. Crossing cattle grids and passing through farm gates, eventually you reach the lighthouse at the end of the cape. Access to the lighthouse itself is barred but you can explore the headland on foot – if you can stand up in the wind. As you drive back towards civilisation, the hills around Monte Toro loom up like a much larger range of mountains than they actually are.

✚ 29D5
🍴 None

CAP DE FAVÀRITX ✪✪

Stand on Menorca's northeastern tip when the *tramuntana* is blowing and you will appreciate the island's savage beauty. Waves crash against crumbling slate cliffs, throwing sea-spray high into the air, and the solitary light-house acts as a reassuring reminder of humanity. The road from Maó is wide at first but eventually deteriorates into a bumpy track which in the end is little more than a causeway across the beach. From the cliffs at the end of the road you look out into an endless Mediterranean Sea. There are several quiet beaches which can be easily reached on foot from here, beginning with Cala Presili (► 63).

✚ 29F4
🍴 None
🔄 Cala Presili (► 63)

A wild goat at Cap de Cavallería: they get used to being photographed

ERMITA DE SANT JOAN DE MISSA

This 15th-century Gothic church, brilliantly whitewashed and visible for miles around, is only used once a year – on the eve of the Festa de Sant Joan (➤ 116), when a horseback procession from Ciutadella rides out for a traditional Mass before returning to the city for the festivities. At other times the church is locked, but if you're on your way to Cala En Turqueta (➤ 59) it's worth stopping to look at the small gabled bell-tower and the ivy branches across the simple arched façade.

ES CASTELL

Founded by the British during their second occupation, and originally named Georgetown after George III, Es Castell retains the feel of a British colonial town. The Spanish renamed it Villacarlos after their own king; locals call it Es Castell because of its proximity to Fort Sant Felip (➤ 76). The main square, Plaça de S'Esplanada, is the former British parade ground, lined with solid Georgian buildings with sash windows and fanlights. Opposite the plum-red town hall, with its British clock tower, is the **Military Museum**, based in the old Cala Corb barracks. It contains a good collection of flags, guns and maps as well as model reconstructions of Fort Sant Felip and some fine 18th-century English furniture.

Es Castell is the most easterly town in Spain and thus the first to get the morning sun. Cales Fonts, a short walk from the main square, is an attractive sheltered harbour where you can dine at one of the many waterfront restaurants or pick up a boat tour of the Port de Maó (➤ 23).

28B3
Only on 23 Jun
None
Cala En Turqueta (➤ 59)
Mass & procession on 23 Jun

29F2
Wide choice of restaurants, mostly in Cales Fonts (££)
Buses from Maó
Port de Maó (➤ 23), Cala de Sant Esteve (➤ 56), Fort Sant Felip (➤ 76)
Market Mon & Wed; Festa de Sant Jaume 24–6 Jul

Military Museum
Plaça de S'Esplanada
Sat–Sun 11–1
Free

The Georgian town hall in the main square of Es Castell

A Walk From Es Castell

Start in Plaça de S'Esplanada, outside the town hall.

Facing the military museum (► 70), head right along Carrer Cales Fonts. Go down into the small harbour of Cala Corb then up the other side to join Carrer Sant Cristòfol. At the end of this road turn left. Cross the roundabout and walk uphill. Turn left at the crossroads; just after passing Carrer des Fusters on the left, take the country lane to your right.

This lane immediately swings left beside a large house, then continues across farmland between walls, eventually reaching a road.

Cross the road and take the track opposite; when this joins another road bear right. Passing a military base, turn left on to a wide track marked Horts de Binissaida. At the end of this track, go left on a walled path – when the wall on your right runs out, climb through a gap and follow the footpath towards the sea. Soon you drop down to Cala de Sant Esteve (► 56), arriving beside the entrance to the Marlborough Redoubt.

Across the creek you see the ruins of Fort Sant Felip (► 76).

Walk around the bay and climb the narrow path at the far end to rejoin the road. Turn right at the cemetery. This road skirts the Sol del Este estate before reaching a small cove. Drop down to the beach then climb up the other side; continue through a modern estate and over another road. Turn right at the T-junction to reach Cales Fonts for lunch; from here, Carrer Stuart leads back to the main square.

Distance
10km

Time
2½ hours plus lunch

Start/end point
Es Castell
🚻 29F2
🚌 Bus from Maó

Lunch
Ca'n Delio (££)
✉ Cales Fonts 38
☎ 35 17 11

The harbour at Cales Fonts is perfectly placed to catch the midday sun

29D3

Bars & restaurants (££)

Buses from Maó & Ciutadella

Monte Toro (► 20)

Festa de Sant Martí, third Sun in Jul

Above: Carrer Major in Es Mercadal – the house with the flags flying is the town hall

ES MERCADAL ✪✪

The name of this town gives away its origins – it was founded in the 14th century as a central market halfway between the ports of Maó and Ciutadella. Much later it was the setting for a defining moment in Menorcan history, when a meeting of his supporters in 1706 declared the Austrian archduke Charles, pretender to the Spanish throne, to be king – providing the pretext for the subsequent British invasion and occupation.

Nowadays Es Mercadal is a quiet town of plain white houses in the shadow of Menorca's highest mountain, Monte Toro (► 20). The main industries are the manufacture of *abarcas*, local sandals with soles made from recycled tyres, and the almond biscuits known as *amargas* and *carquinyols*.

This is the sort of sleepy place that tourism has passed by. Carrer Major, the old main street, is a long pedestrian thoroughfare which climbs gently from the central square past white-walled, green-shuttered houses. At the top of Carrer Major is an old windmill, one of several restaurants in the town specialising in traditional Menorcan cuisine.

ES MIGJORN GRAN ⊕⊕

The name of this quiet village means 'the large town in the south', *es migjorn* being the local term for the low limestone plateau, broken by gorges, which dominates the landscape of southern Menorca. For 200 years the village was known as San Cristóbal, after a blacksmith who founded a township here in 1769 – but before that it was known locally as Es Migjorn Gran and it has recently reverted to its old name.

This is the only one of the inland towns not on the Maó–Ciutadella highway and it retains a certain provincial charm. The main street, Carrer Major, is like a painting of old Menorca – simple white houses with balconies and green shutters, the few houses in bright blues and yellows providing an attractive contrast. During the *siesta* this street is deserted; then at 5PM it suddenly comes to life as ordinary-looking houses turn into shops and bars.

Cova des Coloms

An easy excursion can be made from Es Migjorn Gran to this remarkable cave in the Binigaus gorge. Take the first right after entering the town from Ferreries – you pass a primary school, a *talaiot* and a cemetery – then continue along a track to the farm of Binigaus Vell. Park by the farm gates and walk down the track to your left (marked *cuevas*). Clamber over the wall to your left at another *cuevas* sign and follow the white arrows on the ground, crossing the valley floor to reach the cave. It is dank, dark and atmospheric, the size of a cathedral and buzzing with birds and bats.

🔲 28C3
🍴 Bars & restaurants (£–££)
🚌 Buses from Maó & Ferreries, & a link to Sant Tomàs in summer
↔ Sant Agustí Vell (➤ 82)
❓ Market Wed; Festa de Sant Cristòfol: late Jul/early Aug

The parish church of Sant Cristòfol in Es Migjorn Gran

➕ 28C3

🍴 Lots of restaurants & bars (£–££)

🚌 Buses from Maó & Ciutadella

↔ Binisues (➤ 52)

❓ Market Tue & Fri; Festa de Sant Bartomeu 23–5 Aug

Ferreries has few obvious sights, but that is part of its appeal

FERRERIES ✪✪

The highest town in Menorca – 150m above sea-level – was built in the shadow of the island's second-highest mountain, S'Enclusa. The name of the mountain means 'anvil' and it is thought that the town's name derives from the word for 'blacksmith' – this was probably a centre of smithing along the road from Maó to Ciutadella. The main industries nowadays are furniture and shoe manufacture; there are two factory shops selling high-class leather shoes.

Plaça d'Espanya, at the heart of the town, is a large modern square with a fountain and a children's play area. East and south of here are the wide avenues of the new town, which has expanded greatly since the 1940s; west and north are the narrow streets of a typical Menorcan town, all white houses with green shutters and a 19th-century parish church, Sant Bartomeu, adorned with simple white and cream arches. The town is overlooked from the main road by a fine stairway of *tancas*, or cultivated terraces. Less pretty than its neighbours Es Mercadal and Es Migjorn Gran, it nevertheless retains an honest, lived-in feel – perhaps because the successful local industries mean that it is well-populated throughout the year.

Just outside Ferreries is Son Mercer de Baix, an early Talaiotic village overlooking the confluence of two gorges (see opposite).

FORNELLS (➤ 18, TOP TEN)

A Walk Near Ferreries

This walk takes you deep into a valley for a close-up look at one of Menorca's limestone gorges. It is strenuous but spectacular, and easy to follow.

Start at the farm of Son Mercer de Dalt, 2km from Ferreries and signposted from the road to Es Migjorn Gran (walking from Ferreries will add an hour to the time). Take the track between the farmhouse drive and some barns, signposted Poblat de Son Mercer de Baix. After a few minutes, turn left on to a wide track; this passes through two gates then descends to the valley floor where you enter a lush field.

After five minutes you reach a secluded house. Cross the yard of the house, remembering to shut the gate, and continue on a lane above an orchard. When the lane divides, fork right to climb out of the valley. Climb for 20–30 minutes, then go through a gate; a right turn at the next gate leads into a field and soon you see the farm of Son Mercer de Baix ahead. When you reach a junction with the farm on your right, turn left.

View from the top – looking down from Son Mercer de Baix

The next section is an optional extra but well worth it. An easy walk of around 1km brings you out at the prehistoric village of Son Mercer, where you can picnic among the *talaiots* and look down over the valley to see how far you have climbed.

Return along the same track but continue straight ahead through the farmyard. In the distance you see the impressive farmhouse of Son Mercer de Dalt – your destination.

Distance
8km

Time
2½ hours

Start/end point
Son Mercer de Dalt
✚ 28C3
🚌 Bus to Ferreries then walk for 2km

Lunch
Take a picnic

75

Above: *looking out from Fort Sant Felip towards the headland of La Mola*

Right: *Na Macaret, seen from across the bay*

FORT SANT FELIP ⭐⭐

Not much remains of this once impregnable fortress, begun at the southern entrance to Maó harbour following the Turkish raids in the 16th century. It was the British who strengthened it in the 18th century, using the most modern military engineering techniques to create a network of tunnels which allowed a whole garrison of soldiers to live underground, out of sight of sea-borne invaders. It was here that the British were holed up during the French conquest of 1756; the 83-year-old General Blakeney only surrendered when it became clear that no help would arrive by sea. When the Spanish regained Menorca following the next period of British rule, one of their first acts was to destroy the fort. Whatever the reason, it was a disastrous mistake; the British were able to retake the island in 1798 without the loss of a single life. The fort is still used by the army today; you can visit, but only with a permit from the military authorities. Ask at the Military Museum in Es Castell (➤ 70), which traces the history of the fort and its role in the various battles for Menorca.

MONTE TORO (➤ 20, TOP TEN)

NA MACARET ✪

This old-fashioned seaside village 10km north of Alaior was one of the first Menorcan beach resorts in the 19th century – hence it avoided much of the vulgarity of the resorts that were developed much later. Rows of two-storey waterfront cottages face on to a small, sandy beach and a long narrow inlet which provides a perfect haven for yachts. There has been some recent development but it is relatively restrained.

 29E4
 Two restaurants by the beach (££)
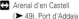 Arenal d'en Castell (➤ 49), Port d'Addaia (➤ 78)

*The attractive marina
at Port d'Addaia*

NAVETA DES TUDONS (► 21, TOP TEN)

PORT D'ADDAIA

Menorca's third-longest natural harbour, more than 3km long and 400m wide, is popular with the yachting set because of the protection it provides from the *tramuntana* wind. John Armstrong, who wrote the first English guide to Menorca in 1752, described this as the most perfect place on the island, and it is certainly very attractive. From the marina you look out across the masts of the yachts to a long, woody inlet and a sea framed by cliffs and small islands. This was the site of the final British invasion of Menorca in 1798, when Britain managed to capture the island without loss of life following the destruction of Fort Sant Felip by the Spanish. Inevitably a resort has mushroomed above the marina but the waterside itself remains blissfully unspoilt.

PUNTA NATI

Drive out here on a windy day – or better still, take a bike – and you will see why Menorca is called an island of stones and wind. The 6km road to the island's northwestern tip has little to offer apart from endless vistas of a barren, rocky landscape punctuated by stepped *ponts*, the drystone sheep and cattle sheds which protect the livestock from the extremes of the weather and help clear the fields of unwanted stones. On the wind-buffeted headland, as ever, the lighthouse is off limits, but you can walk along the cliffs to a couple of deserted coves.

PUNTA PRIMA ⭐

The southeastern extremity of Menorca boasts one of the island's largest and finest beaches – but the currents in this part of Menorca can be dangerous and swimmers should pay particular attention to the Red Cross flag and only swim if the green flag is flying.

This is a popular area for watersports – you can hire windsurfing and sailing equipment, as well as pedal boats, on the beach. Facing Punta Prima across the sea is the Illa de l'Aire, an uninhabited island with an automatic lighthouse, clear sea-beds for diving and a small harbour for yachts. The island is the home of a rare species of black lizard.

🔲 29F1
🍴 Restaurants & bars
(£–££)
🚌 Buses from Maó & Sant Lluís in summer

Above: *timeless pleasures on the beach at Punta Prima*

RAFAL RUBÍ NOU ⭐

Most people head for the Naveta des Tudons (➤ 21) to see the best-preserved example of a burial *naveta*; but it can be just as exciting to discover the lesser Bronze Age sites away from the beaten path. Signposted down a country lane on the main highway 6.7km west of Maó, Rafal Rubí consists of two *navetas* set in the middle of farmland.

🔲 29E2
🔵 Free access
🍴 None
↔ Talatí de Dalt (➤ 88)

S'ABUFERA DES GRAU (➤ 24, TOP TEN)

Did you know ?

When the British governor was under siege from the French in Fort Sant Felip in 1756, a fleet of ships under Admiral Byng sailed from Gibraltar to protect him. They reached the Illa de l'Aire and were all set to proceed on Maó harbour; but they turned and fled back to Gibraltar instead. The British surrendered; Byng was court-martialled and shot 'to encourage the others', as Voltaire put it.

Above: *a limestone cathedral – the quarry at S'Hostal near Ciutadella*

S'HOSTAL ○○

Menorca's most unusual tourist attraction is a disused limestone quarry outside Ciutadella which has been turned into a monument to the island's history and traditions of quarrying. Limestone has been used for building since prehistoric times; soft and permeable, hence easy to extract, it turns hard when exposed to the air and is the perfect building material. Traditionally it was extracted by hammer and chisel; the few remaining quarries use circular saws which dig deep into the ground, creating vertical walls of white stone.

The quarry closed in 1994; it was bought up by Líthica and reopened the following year. You can walk around a 'labyrinth of orchards' in the old quarry, now being turned into a garden, then descend to the giant white amphitheatre of the modern quarry, 30m deep, where on weekdays workmen give displays of quarrying and at other times you stand in the eerie quiet of a limestone cathedral. Líthica has ambitious plans for this site – a limestone sculpture park, a museum and visitor centre, a concert auditorium beneath the sheer white walls. An industrial wasteland has been creatively transformed into an unexpectedly special place.

SA TORRETA ○

One of the few Talaiotic sites in northern Menorca is also one of the hardest to reach; the best way is the walk from Es Grau (➤ facing page). Overgrown and evocative, a complete *taula* 4m high is surrounded by standing stones on the edge of a farm. Tests show that this was built 1,000 years after the *taulas* at Son Catlar (➤ 86) and Trepucó (➤ 90) – so the Talaiotic culture was certainly not short-lived.

A Coastal Walk to Sa Torreta

This walk has everything – countryside, archaeology, beaches and coastal views.

Begin at Es Grau (▶ 24), walking around the beach to the far side opposite the car park. Climb the footpath on to the cliffs and turn right. Ignore all junctions and continue until you see Illa d'en Colom ahead. Follow the path down towards the sea, passing a cave house and crossing behind a small beach.

The path now swings left to cross a headland and drops to Fondeadero de los Llanes.

Walk around this bay, passing two inlets and a sandy beach, then up a slope on the far side where a narrow path leads through a gap in a wall to join a cart-track. Note this spot carefully – there is a red arrow on a stone to guide you – and turn left.

An easy circular walk returns you to this spot. The track skirts the S'Albufera lagoon then climbs to Sa Torreta farm after 30–40 minutes.

At the farm, an overgrown path beside a concrete barn leads to Sa Torreta (▶ facing page). Returning to the farmyard, turn left, ie right if you had not visited the taula. The track descends to Cala de Sa Torreta, shaded by pine woods, then climbs above the bay, passing another beach before turning inland. Now look for the junction where you began the circular walk. Turn left to return to Es Grau by the same route.

At Es Grau beach, go through the gap between the dunes to cross part of the S'Albufera reserve. You emerge on the main road a few minutes south of the village.

Distance
11km

Time
3 hours plus picnic

Start/end point
Es Grau
✚ 29F3
🚌 Buses from Maó in summer

Lunch
Take a picnic

The walk from Es Grau leads along a wild section of the coast

➕ 28C2
🍴 Beach bar in summer;
restaurants at Sant
Tomàs (££)
🚌 Buses to Sant Tomàs
from Maó, Ciutadella &
Es Migjorn Gran in
summer
↔ Sant Tomàs (► 84)

SANT ADEODATO ✪

The western end of Sant Tomàs beach (► 84), beyond the road from Es Migjorn Gran, is totally undeveloped and known as Sant Adeodato. The sand is fine, the swimming is safe but there are few beach facilities. A short walk on a sandy path behind the beach, passing the islet of Binicodrell offshore, brings you to the larger beach at Binigaus, popular with nudists but with dangerous currents which make it unsafe for swimming. From Binigaus you can walk inland along the Barranc de Binigaus, a limestone gorge riddled with caves, including the cathedral-like Cova des Coloms – though the easier approach to this particular cave is from Es Migjorn Gran (► 73).

➕ 28C3
⊘ Free access
🍴 None
🚌 Buses to Es Migjorn Gran
from Maó & Ferreries
↔ Es Migjorn Gran (► 73)

SANT AGUSTÍ VELL ✪

This is one of the hardest of Menorca's prehistoric sites to find but that makes the effort all the more rewarding and you will probably be alone with your thoughts when you get there. Take the road from Es Migjorn Gran to Sant Tomàs; after 1km, an unsigned track to your right leads to the farm of Sant Agustí. At the farm gates, go right, through a gate marked *cuevas*; when you see a pair of litter bins you know that you have reached the site. The main attraction here is a large *talaiot* with a beamed roof of olive and juniper wood; once they would all have been like this but this is the only one which survives. The village was strategically situated at the head of the Binigaus gorge, and the *cuevas* referred to include the Cova d'en Coloms – though this is more easily reached by returning to Es Migjorn Gran (► 73).

Above: *the quiet beach
at Sant Adeodato is
dwarfed by its neighbour,
Sant Tomàs*

SANT CLIMENT ✪

Unusually for the Mediterranean, this is a self-contained community where many locals grew up in the village and have lived there ever since – though most now work in Maó or at the airport, just a Balearic slingshot away. The village has two bars, a chemist, a baker, a newsagent and a mini-market, plus the inevitable main square with palm trees at its corners and an 18th-century church with a 20th-century façade.

+ 29E2
❢ Bars (£) & Casino San Clemente (££)
🚌 Buses from Maó
↔ Torelló (▶ 88)
❓ Festa de Sant Climent – third weekend in Aug

SANT LLUÍS ✪✪

Even by Menorcan standards, Sant Lluís is white – when the sun is shining, it fairly sparkles. Founded by the French in 1761 during their brief occupation of Menorca to provide housing for their troops, it is laid out in a grid style around a series of attractive squares. The town was named after Louis IX, to whom the huge, whitewashed, buttressed church is dedicated; the west front contains the coats of arms of the French royal family as well as the Comte de Lannion, Menorca's first French governor.

A blue and white windmill, **Molí de Dalt**, seen as you enter the town from Maó, has been turned into a small folk museum with a collection of old farm implements – the main square opposite the windmill contains a good children's playground. Despite having become virtually a suburb of Maó, Sant Lluís remains a quiet, pretty town with a laid-back atmosphere and, perhaps surprisingly given its origins, a large British community. The hamlet of Torret to the south contains some of the finest traditional rural houses on the island.

+ 29E2
❢ Restaurants & bars (££)
🚌 Buses from Maó
❓ Festa de Sant Lluís – last weekend in Aug

Molí de Dalt
☎ 15 10 84
🕐 Wed–Mon 10–1, 6:30–8:30 in summer; Mon/ Wed/ Thu/ Fri 11–2, Sat 9–12, Sun 10–1 in winter
💷 Cheap

The Molí de Dalt windmill announces your arrival in Sant Lluís

SANT TOMÀS ✪

28C2
🍴 Restaurants & bars (££)
🚌 Buses from Maó, Ciutadella & Es Migjorn Gran in summer
↔ Sant Adeodato (➤ 82)

This long beach of pale golden sand is virtually a continuation of the beach at Son Bou (➤ 25), separated from it by a pair of low headlands. Once a quiet spot, it has grown into a major resort with four large hotels and an *urbanización* creeping up the hills behind the beach. In 1989 a freak storm blew away all the sand from the beach and what you see now has been imported in its place. A path at the western end of the beach leads to the quieter beaches of Sant Adeodato and Binigaus (➤ 82). Take note of the flag system for safe bathing as the beach has dangerous currents.

SANTA AGUEDA ✪✪

28C4
🍴 None
↔ Binisues (➤ 52)

Climbing Menorca's third-highest hill today, there is little to suggest that it once supported the island's most significant fortress. Built by the Romans and strengthened by the Moors, the castle on Santa Agueda's summit was the last Muslim stronghold to resist the Catalan conquest in 1287.

The buildings have fallen into disrepair and only the serious archaeologist would recognise the Roman, Arab and Spanish influences – but it is still worth the walk up here for the views, which stretch to both Maó and Ciutadella and along the windswept north coast. As a bonus, the path to the summit takes you along the best-preserved Roman road in Menorca. To get there, take the Binisues road, signposted off the C721 3km west of Ferreries; after another 3km, park by an old white schoolhouse and go through the gate to begin your walk. The climb to the summit takes a brisk 20–30 minutes. This is a popular picnic spot, much used by local families at weekends.

SHANGRI-LA ⭐

The name means 'an imaginary paradise', and imaginary it has turned out to be. Conceived in the tourist boom of the 1970s as an up-market golf resort on the shores of the S'Albufera lake (➤ 24), Shangri-La was the subject of years of legal and political argument before being finally halted on the grounds that it represented illegal development in a conservation area. By this time many of the houses had been built; some were already lived in. The victory for Menorca's environmental campaigners proved to be a landmark, as the island realised that mass tourism had to be controlled if it was not to go the way of neighbouring Mallorca. But a half-built *urbanización* is even worse than a finished one, and if you wander around Shangri-La today you are bound to be struck by the air of sadness and desolation, with the golf course overgrown, the roads unmade and villas abandoned when the money ran out. It serves as a lesson to anyone else tempted to create a new 'village' and call it paradise.

🚌 29E3
🍴 None
🚍 Buses from Maó to Es Grau in summer
🔁 S'Albufera d'es Grau (➤ 24)

Above: *life is non-stop fun at the Club San Jaime near Son Bou*

SO NA CAÇANA ⭐

A short walk south of Torre Llisà Vell (➤ 90) on the Alaior to Cala En Porter road, this Bronze Age site with two *talaiots* and two *taulas* – both with their horizontal stone missing – is one of Menorca's least-visited archaeological sites. It is certainly not worth a detour, but if you have got out of your car already to see Torre Llisà Vell you may want to combine the two. Get there through a gap in the wall beside the main road.

🚌 29D2
⭕ Free access
🍴 None
🔁 Torralba d'en Salord (➤ 89), Torre Llisà Vell (➤ 90)

Opposite: *a well-preserved Roman road leads to the summit of Santa Agueda*

SON BOU (➤ 25, TOP TEN)

Was it built by giants? The outer wall of Son Catlar

28B3
Free access
None
Arenal de Son Saura
(► 49)

SON CATLAR ✪✪

Menorca's largest megalithic settlement is reached on the road from Ciutadella to Arenal de Son Saura. Built around 1800 BC, it grew to its present size in Roman times and continued to be occupied right up to the Middle Ages. The most impressive feature here is the surrounding wall, some 900m in circumference and built of massive stones – walls such as this one are often known as Cyclopean because of the belief that only giants could have built them. A doorway at the north side of the wall leads to a *taula* precinct, but the horizontal stone on top of the *taula* has fallen and collapsed. Unlike most prehistoric sites on Menorca, Son Catlar has helpful, multi-lingual information boards to guide you around.

29D4
Bars & restaurants
(£–££), including beach
bar in summer
Buses from Maó &
Fornells in summer

SON PARC ✪✪

A dreary *urbanización*, with a golf course and hundreds of identical apartments, leads to this perfect beach, which is large enough not to get too crowded even in high summer. The water is shallow, there are pedaloes and motorboats for hire, and the dunes and pine woods at the back of the beach offer some relief from the sun. As so often in Menorca, there is also a peaceful cove just a short walk away from a busy resort. Take the path through a gap in the wall at the west end of the beach, walk for 20 minutes across the headland breathing in the pungent mix of wild rosemary and salty sea breeze, cross a shingle beach, climb a hillock and then drop to Cala Pudent where, out of season, you can have the beach to yourself.

DRIVE

A Drive Along the Camí d'en Kane

When the British moved the capital to Maó, they also built a new road from Maó to Ciutadella – financed by a tax on alcohol. Parts of the road, named after the first British governor, still exist and have been restored.

Start by the ferry station on the waterfront at Maó. Take the road north for Fornells. Shortly after leaving the harbour you pass a monument to Sir Richard Kane on your right. After another 2km, turn left on to a quiet country road, the Camí d'en Kane.

This road rises and falls through typical Menorcan countryside – meadows, cattle, drystone walls. After 9km you see the town of Alaior to your left and a cemetery on your right.

Keep straight ahead as the road narrows and passes beneath a canopy of pine trees.

Monte Toro rises up ahead of you – a recurring feature of the next few kilometres. Eventually Camí d'en Kane ends and you join the main highway from Maó to Ciutadella (from here it roughly follows the route of Kane's original road).

Turn right and almost immediately right again, skirting the town of Es Mercadal and following signs to Fornells.

Continue to this beautiful fishing village (➤ 18) for lunch by the harbour.

Leave Fornells by the same road; after 3km, turn left towards Maó.

This road passes through some of Menorca's most thickly wooded areas before returning to Maó harbour. Several roads to the left lead to various north coast resorts, including Arenal d'en Castell (➤ 49) and Son Parc (➤ facing page).

Distance
56km

Time
1½ hours plus lunch

Start point
Maó harbour
29F2

End point
Maó

Lunch
Es Passeig Marítim (££)
Passeig Marítim, Fornells
37 63 12

View along the Camí d'en Kane

TALATÍ DE DALT ⭐⭐

29E2

Signposted off the Maó–Ciutadella road, 4km from Maó

Free access

None

Rafal Rubí Nou (➤ 79), Torelló (see below)

Like many of Menorca's prehistoric monuments, Talatí de Dalt blends so well into its surroundings that it is difficult to tell which of the piles of stones are ancient and which modern. A wild olive tree grows inside the *taula* precinct; bushes sprout out of a *talaiot* and standing stones are scattered around a field. The central *taula* is one of the largest in Menorca; a separate pillar leans against it, probably a result of an accident. The site dates from 1400 BC, but it was inhabited until at least Roman times.

TORELLÓ ⭐⭐

29E2

Off the Maó–Sant Climent road

Free access

None

Sant Climent (➤ 83), Talatí de Dalt (see above)

Two sites separated by 300m and a millennium of history are found in the shadow of a modern airport. The *talaiot* here, one of the largest in Menorca, is often the first that visitors see – it is visible from incoming planes.

Of more interest is the 6th-century basilica, Es Fornàs de Torelló, discovered in 1956 by a farmer ploughing up his fields. The church, built under Byzantine rule, is protected by a corrugated iron roof – but you can walk around the viewing platform and marvel at the motifs of peacocks, lions and palm trees on the mosaic floor. Parts of the altar survive, as does the baptismal font; the design suggests an African influence, indicating early links with the North African church.

Above: *an ancient chamber at Talatí de Dalt*

TORRALBA D'EN SALORD

This extensive site, 3km south of Alaior, is the closest Menorca has come to turning its prehistoric ruins into a tourist attraction. The road which used to bisect the site has been diverted, a large car and coach park created, and wooden arrows have been put up to guide visitors around Menorca's first archaeological park. There are the remains of a complete village here, including a *taula*, a *talaiot* and a remarkable well, 46m deep with nine flights of steps and a stone handrail hewn out of the rock. From the village there are good views of the white town of Alaior with Monte Toro (➤ 20) towering over it in the distance.

TORRE D'EN GAUMÉS (➤ 26, TOP TEN)

TORRE LLAFUDA

This little-visited site off the highway from Maó to Ciutadella contains a complete *taula*, less than 2m tall and romantically surrounded by a halo of wild olive and holm oak. Near the *taula* are a set of burial caves and some well-preserved defensive walls. Among the finds here was a Roman gold ring engraved with the figure of a camel; like many prehistoric sites, Torre Llafuda continued to be occupied well into Roman times and possibly much later.

✚	29D2
⊠	On the Alaior–Cala En Porter road
🕐	Free access
🍴	Refreshment hut in summer
↔	Alaior (➤ 48), Torre Llisà Vell (➤ 90)

✚	28B3
⊠	Signposted off the Maó–Ciutadella road at 37km
🕐	Free access
🍴	None
↔	Naveta des Tudons (➤ 21)

Did you know ?

One of the objects found at Torralba d'en Salord was a bronze figure of a calf – suggesting that the bull was venerated in Menorca in ancient times as it was elsewhere in the Mediterranean. One of the many theories about taulas is that they may have been worshipped as stylised images of bulls.

Above: *excavations at Torralba d'en Salord suggest that the site was used for ritual animal sacrifices*

TORRE LLISÀ VELL ⊕

This is the sort of place that makes seeking out Menorca's ancient monuments worthwhile – even if you have no interest in archaeology. Turn right off the Alaior to Cala En Porter road 5km south of Alaior at the crossroads marked 'Camí de Cutaines'; park at the farm and follow red arrows through the fields to reach the *taula* precinct, enclosed by its original wall. A perfectly preserved stone archway, perhaps 3,000 years old, guards the precinct – as you stoop beneath the ancient arch you wonder just how many people have stood there before you and why.

29D2
⊙ Free access
⊪ None
↔ So Na Caçana (► 85), Torralba d'en Salord (► 89)

TORRE TRENCADA ⊕

Drive across farmland on the old Roman road from Ciutadella to Maó, turn into a small car park, cross two cattle grids and across a field you catch sight of a monumental *taula* hiding among the trees. Birds sing and cattle graze as you cross the field; the prehistoric village is surrounded by drystone walls and as with so many of Menorca's ancient sites it is hard to tell where the old stones end and the new ones begin.

28B3
⊙ Free access
⊪ None
↔ S'Hostal (► 80)

TREPUCÓ ⊕⊕

On the outskirts of Maó are a massive *taula* and *talaiot* which have stood for 3,000 years while invaders have come and gone. The *taula* here, 4m high, is the tallest in Menorca. The complex is surrounded by a star-shaped wall, built by the Duc de Crillon in 1782 when the French were laying siege to Fort Sant Felip (► 76) and used Trepucó as their base. In 1931 the site was excavated by Margaret Murray, who found small boys playing on top of the overgrown *taula*. A notice asks visitors not to climb on the ruins.

29F2
✉ Signposted off the Maó–Sant Lluis road
⊙ Free access
⊪ None
↔ Maó (► 30)

The taula *and* talaiot *at Trepucó*

Where To...

Maó

Prices

Prices are approximate, based on a three-course meal for one without drinks and service:

£ = under 2,000 ptas
££ = 2,000–4,000 ptas
£££ = over 4,000 ptas

Most restaurants serve a *menú del día* (➤ 95) at lunchtime (and sometimes in the evening) which will usually work out much cheaper. It is normal practice to add about 10 per cent to the bill as a tip.

Alba (££)

Homely Spanish and Italian cuisine with views of the King's Island.

✉ **Moll de Llevant 298** ☎ **35 06 06** ⏰ **Lunch & dinner**

American Bar (£)

Busy meeting-place in the heart of the pedestrian shopping district.

✉ **Plaça Reial 8** ☎ **36 18 22** ⏰ **All day**

Ca'n Nito (££)

Fresh fish and lobster near the foot of the harbour steps.

✉ **Moll de Llevant 15** ☎ **36 52 26** ⏰ **Lunch & dinner. Closed Sun in winter**

Capri (££)

In the basement of the Hotel Capri; specialises in pizzas, cooked in a wood-fired oven.

✉ **Carrer Sant Esteve 8** ☎ **36 80 12** ⏰ **Lunch & dinner**

Casa Sexto (££)

Fishy *tapas* and seafood specialities – the owner flies in fresh seafood from his native Galicia and cooks it in sea water while you wait.

✉ **Carrer Vassallo 2** ☎ **36 84 07** ⏰ **Lunch & dinner. Closed Sun dinner, Mon**

Club Marítimo (££)

The focus of social life among the yacht set at Cala Figuera; *tapas* and pizzas downstairs, a terrace restaurant above.

✉ **Moll de Llevant 287** ☎ **36 42 26** ⏰ **Lunch & dinner**

Consey (£)

Standard international fare in a corner of the city's main square.

✉ **Plaça de S'Esplanada 72** ☎ **36 05 26** ⏰ **All day**

Europa (£)

Small, seedy *tapas* bar close to Plaça de S'Esplanada, with portions of everything from octopus with onions to baked pumpkin and garlic snails.

✉ **Carrer de Cifuentes (Sa Rovellada de Dalt) 68** ☎ **36 13 79** ⏰ **All day**

Gregal (££)

Locals consider this among the best of the harbourside restaurants in Cala Figuera.

✉ **Moll de Llevant 306** ☎ **36 66 06** ⏰ **Lunch & dinner**

Il Porto (££)

Pizzas and barbecues in an open-plan setting.

✉ **Moll de Llevant 225** ☎ **36 30 38** ⏰ **Lunch & dinner**

Itake (££)

One of the few waterfront restaurants not to concentrate on fish. Fashionable and offbeat.

✉ **Moll de Llevant 317** ☎ **35 45 70** ⏰ **Lunch & dinner. Closed Mon**

L'Arpó (££)

Pretty waterfront bistro specialising in simple fresh fish and *paella*.

✉ **Moll de Llevant 124** ☎ **36 98 44** ⏰ **Lunch & dinner**

La Minerva (££)

Six different dining-rooms and a floating terrace; *nouvelle cuisine*, Menorcan style.

✉ **Moll de Llevant 87** ☎ **35 19 95** ⏰ **Lunch & dinner**

La Tropical (££)

One of the few good restaurants in the city centre; includes a daily 'menu from the market'.

✉ **Carrer La Lluna 36** ☎ **36 05 56** ⏰ **Lunch & dinner**

Latitud 40° (££)
Trendy waterfront restaurant specialising in fresh pasta and seafood.
✉ Moll de Llevant 265 ☎ 36 41 76 🕐 Lunch & dinner

Llevant (££)
A genuine Greek restaurant right beside the harbour.
✉ Moll de Llevant 302 ☎ 36 16 05 🕐 Lunch & dinner

Marivent (£££)
Probably the best of the numerous harbourside restaurants at Cala Figuera.
✉ Moll de Llevant 314 ☎ 36 90 67 🕐 Lunch & dinner

Meson del Puerto (££)
Classic Basque cuisine in a lively area beside the ferry port.
✉ Moll de Ponent 66 ☎ 35 29 03 🕐 Lunch & dinner

Mos i Glop (£)
Simple Menorcan dishes like stuffed vegetables, plus grilled fish and – unusually – *paella* for one.
✉ Carrer Alaior 12 ☎ 36 64 57 🕐 Lunch & dinner. Closed Sun

Nashville (££)
The ultimate in cultural confusion – pizzas, German and Tex-Mex dishes in this 'beer and soundhouse' down by the sea.
✉ Moll de Llevant 145 ☎ 36 79 56 🕐 Lunch & dinner. Closed Mon in winter

Pans i Pans (£)
Menorcan branch of a well-known Spanish chain specialising in pizzas and baguettes. Popular with young people in the evening.
✉ Plaça de S'Esplanada 31 ☎ 35 10 68 🕐 All day

Pasarela (££)
A wide range of *tapas* plus fresh fish and seafood, and a hearty Castilian menu which changes daily.
✉ Moll de Ponent 25 ☎ 36 95 19 🕐 Lunch & dinner. Closed Mon

Passage to India (££)
Waterfront restaurant specialising in tandoori and other Indian dishes.
✉ Moll de Ponent 28 ☎ 35 35 91 🕐 Lunch & dinner

Pilar (£££)
Charming family-run restaurant with a garden terrace and an innovative menu.
✉ Carrer des Forn 61 ☎ 36 68 17 🕐 Dinner only

Roma (£)
Fashionable, reasonably priced pizzeria among the smart restaurants in Cala Figuera.
✉ Moll de Llevant 295 ☎ 35 37 77 🕐 Lunch & dinner. Closed Thu lunch

S'Espigo (££)
Small, stylish restaurant with a wide range of fish baked in sea salt.
✉ Moll de Llevant 267 ☎ 36 99 09 🕐 Lunch & dinner

Sa Parada (£)
Good-value *tapas* and set lunch on a shady terrace.
✉ Plaça de S'Esplanada 64 ☎ 36 52 13 🕐 All day

San José (££)
British-run farmhouse restaurant on the Fornells road. Advanced booking necessary.
✉ Carretera Maó–Fornells ☎ 35 17 59 🕐 Dinner Mon–Sat, Sun lunch

Opening Times
The Spanish like to eat late – many restaurants do not even open until 1:30 at lunchtime and 8:30 in the evening, and fill up an hour or two later. Most restaurants either close down for the winter or severely reduce their opening times, so it is always a good idea to check in advance. *Tapas* bars tend to be open throughout the day.

Ciutadella

Tapas

Tapas are a Spanish institution. Originally a free 'lid' (*tapa*) of ham across a drink, nowadays they consist of small portions of everything from octopus to olives. Locals tend to eat *tapas* before going home for dinner, but several portions can make a filling meal in itself. And you don't have to look at a menu – just point to what you want in the cabinet.

Aurora (£)
Simple Menorcan cuisine on a lively square where the old town meets the new.
✉ Plaça Alfons III 1 ☎ 38 00 29 🕐 Lunch & dinner

Burger King (£)
Menorca's first branch of this international fast-food chain.
✉ Plaça des Born 2 🕐 All day in summer; dinner Fri–Sun in winter

Café Balear (££)
The perfect setting for lunch; plenty of fresh shellfish plus steaks and *carpaccio* of veal.
✉ Passeig de Sant Joan 17 ☎ 38 00 05 🕐 Lunch & dinner

Ca'n Nito (££)
Tapas bar on the edge of the Born with lots of fish dishes and steaks.
✉ Plaça des Born 11 🕐 All day

Ca's Quinto (££)
Excellent seafood *tapas* plus a lengthy fish menu. Popular with locals and tourists alike.
✉ Plaça Alfons III 3 ☎ 38 10 02 🕐 Lunch & dinner

Casa Manolo (£££)
Top-notch fresh seafood and lobster dishes beside the harbour walls.
✉ Carrer Marina 117 ☎ 38 00 03 🕐 Lunch & dinner

Chinatown Two (££)
The set menu at this Cantonese restaurant is one of the best bargains in town.
✉ Carrer Mallorca 34 ☎ 48 08 71 🕐 Lunch & dinner

Club Náutico (££)
Serious fish dishes; overlooks the entrance to the port.
✉ Camí Baix, beneath Passeig Marítim ☎ 38 11 46 🕐 Lunch & dinner

Corb Marí (££)
One of several fish restaurants lining the harbour.
✉ Carrer Marina 43 ☎ 38 42 93 🕐 Lunch & dinner

El Bribón (££)
Down by the harbour it's a question of just taking your pick, but this seafood restaurant and *tapas* bar is better value than most.
✉ Carrer Marina 115 ☎ 38 50 50 🕐 Lunch & dinner

El Comilón (££)
French-style restaurant and *crêperie*.
✉ Plaça de S'Esplanada 48 ☎ 38 09 22 🕐 Lunch & dinner

El Horno (££)
Intimate basement restaurant near the Plaça des Born.
✉ Carrer des Forn 10 ☎ 38 07 67 🕐 Dinner only

Es Fabiol (£)
A branch of the Ses Voltes string of restaurant-bars in Ciutadella, specialising in pizzas, baguettes and Menorcan sausages.
✉ Plaça de S'Esplanada ☎ 48 23 70 🕐 Lunch & dinner

Es Moll (££)
Some of the freshest fish you'll ever find in a beautiful setting beside the harbour. The lunchtime *menú del día* is especially good value.
✉ Moll Commercial ☎ 48 08 13 🕐 Lunch & dinner

Il Palato Fino (££)

Popular Italian restaurant with home-made bread, fresh pasta and a range of set menus.

✉ Carrer Sant Isidro 15 ☎ 38 55 15 🕐 Lunch & dinner

La Guitarra (££)

Classic Menorcan dishes – duck, roast lamb, stuffed squid – in an atmospheric cellar.

✉ Carrer Nostra Senyora dels Dolors 1 ☎ 38 13 55 🕐 Lunch & dinner

La Mamma (££)

Italian-style *trattoria* featuring classics like steak and *osso bucco*, and pizzas to eat in or take away.

✉ Avinguda Conqueridor 71 ☎ 48 15 97 🕐 Lunch & dinner

La Payesa (££)

A large choice of seafood dishes including three different *paellas*, plus a children's menu featuring burgers, chicken and chips.

✉ Carrer Marina 65 ☎ 38 00 21 🕐 Lunch & dinner

Las Terrazas (££)

Menorcan and Spanish cuisine on a pretty terrace with sea views

✉ Avinguda Ascunción, Cala Busquets ☎ 38 21 58 🕐 Lunch Tue–Sun, dinner Tue–Sat

Menjars des Born (£)

Nothing but simple *tapas* and rolls, but in a prime position on the Born.

✉ Plaça des Born 29 ☎ 38 41 82 🕐 All day

Oristano (£)

Fresh pasta and wood-fired pizzas in an old shoe factory overlooking the Pla de Sant Joan. Popular with a young late-night crowd at weekends.

✉ Carrer Borja Moll 1 ☎ 38 41 97 🕐 Dinner only

Portofino (££)

An eclectic range of pizzas – including dessert pizzas made with yoghurt – overlooking the marina.

✉ Moll Commercial 🕐 Lunch & dinner

Racó des Palau (££)

Fish, pizzas and Italian cuisine in the back streets behind the Palau Salord.

✉ Carrer des Palau 35 ☎ 38 54 02 🕐 Lunch & dinner

Roma (££)

Part of the Café Balear chain, the speciality here is pizzas cooked in a wood-fired oven. Also Italian meat and fish dishes and fresh pasta.

✉ Carrer Pere d'Alcántara 18 ☎ 38 47 18 🕐 Lunch & dinner

Sa Figuera (£££)

Grilled steaks and seafood dishes, including *caldereta de langosta*.

✉ Carrer Marina 99 ☎ 48 20 44 🕐 Lunch & dinner

S'Esplanada (££)

Pasta and pizzas beneath a palm tree on a lively square.

✉ Plaça de S'Esplanada 2 🕐 Lunch & dinner

Ses Voltes (££)

Charcoal-grilled meats, wood-fired pizzas and a dozen varieties of *pa amb oli* (toast with olive oil) are the specialities at this busy café-bar in the pedestrian heart of the city.

✉ Carrer JM Quadrado 22 (Ses Voltes) 🕐 Lunch & dinner

Menú del Día

By law, all restaurants offer a *menú del día* at lunchtime, and many in the evening too – a set-price three-course meal, with water or wine included. You won't get much choice (typically two or three choices for each course) but what you do get will be cheap, freshly cooked and filling. A full meal, with drinks, will usually cost about the same as a main course from the *à la carte* menu.

95

Around the Island

Vegetarians

Vegetarians could have a hard time in Menorca – unless they eat fish. *Tapas* bars, however, usually have vegetarian options, including the ever-present *tortilla* (cold potato omelette), and Menorcan pizzas tend to be excellent, cooked the Italian way in a wood-fired oven. Two interesting vegetarian starters are *escalivada*, a mix of grilled vegetables in olive oil, and *tumbet*, a Mallorcan-style ratatouille with potatoes.

Alaior

Es Plans (££)

English-run restaurant just outside Alaior, with fish and chips on a Friday night and a traditional Sunday lunch.

✉ **Carretera Maó-Ciutadella** ☎ **37 80 78** 🕔 **Dinner daily, Sun lunch**

The Cobblers (££)

Fresh, imaginative Mediterranean cuisine in the garden of a typical Menorcan town house. Booking essential.

✉ **Costa d'en Macari 6** ☎ **37 14 00** 🕔 **Dinner only. Closed Sun**

Ximènes (££)

Cellar restaurant with friendly service and Menorcan home cooking.

✉ **Carrer Dr Albiñana 2** ☎ **37 11 20** 🕔 **Lunch & dinner**

Binibeca Vell

Los Bucaneros (££)

Simple fish restaurant in a wooden shack on the beach. Very romantic.

✉ **Binibeca beach** ☎ **No telephone** 🕔 **Lunch only**

Cala Blanca

Es Caliu (££)

A large and busy restaurant specialising in charcoal-grilled meats.

✉ **Carretera Ciutadella-Cala En Bosc** ☎ **38 01 65** 🕔 **Lunch & dinner**

Los Toboganes (££)

Family restaurant overlooking the beach, with mini-golf and a toboggan slope for the children.

✉ **Cala Blanca beach** ☎ **38 51 68** 🕔 **Lunch & dinner**

Cala En Blanes

Bailey's (££)

English restaurant with traditional and modern food and a range of English beers.

✉ **Carretera Ciutadella-Cala En Blanes** ☎ **48 29 04** 🕔 **Dinner only, 5pm–late**

Cala En Bosc

El Pescador (££)

Fish, pizzas and international food in this busy restaurant beside the marina.

✉ **Marina** ☎ **37 65 38** 🕔 **Lunch & dinner**

Cala En Porter

Noche Noche (££)

Family bar and restaurant with a swimming-pool and a shady terrace. Steak and fish dishes, and a special children's menu.

✉ **Avinguda Central 122** ☎ **37 74 63** 🕔 **Lunch & dinner**

Cala Mesquida

Es Cap Roig (££)

Fresh fish, simply cooked, in a spectacular setting looking out to sea. This is where the people of Maó come for a treat at weekends.

✉ **Just before the village on the road from Maó** ☎ **18 83 83** 🕔 **Lunch & dinner**

Cala Santa Galdana

El Mirador (££)

Perched on a rocky outcrop above one of Menorca's prettiest bays. A wide-ranging menu with the emphasis on seafood.

✉ **Over footbridge from Hotel Audax** ☎ **908 799 847** 🕔 **Lunch & dinner**

Es Castell

Bobbie's Bistro Bar (£)

The '3Bs' caters to an expatriate community homesick for hot dogs, beans and chips. Even the fish here is imported English cod.

Cales Fonts 36 ☎ 35 13
68 🕐 All day

Bumerang (££)
Long-established restaurant
set in an ancient cave.
Paellas, fish dishes and a
good-value set lunch.
✉ Carrer Sant Josep 9 ☎ 36
46 15 🕐 Lunch & dinner

Ca'n Delio (££)
A good place to while away a
summer evening eating fresh
grilled fish beside the sea.
✉ Cales Fonts 38 ☎ 35 17 11
🕐 Lunch & dinner

Ca'n Mito (££)
Great seafood specialities
including octopus, mussels
and sea snails.
✉ Carrer Cala Fonts 12
🕐 Lunch & dinner

Club Náutico (££)
Fresh fish and fine views
over Maó harbour.
✉ Carrer General Mola; steps
up from Cales Fonts ☎ 36 58
84 🕐 Lunch & dinner

El Italiano (££)
Classic Italian cooking in a
country house – risottos,
cheese fondues, pasta with
truffles, Spanish and Italian
wines. Children can ask for
half portions.
✉ Carretera Sant Felip ☎ 36
53 10 🕐 Lunch & dinner

El Trébol (££)
The best-known fish
restaurant in Es Castell, and
a night-time haunt of visiting
celebrities. Offers a sunny
terrace or a shady cave.
✉ Cales Fonts 43 ☎ 36 70 97
🕐 Lunch & dinner

España (£)
The locals come here for
solid, unpretentious

Menorcan food.
✉ Carrer Victori 40 ☎ 36 32
99 🕐 Lunch & dinner

Irene (££)
This restaurant would be
much busier if it were down
by the water. Spanish
cooking with set menus
lunchtime and evening.
✉ Carrer Sa Font 1 ☎ 36 42
04 🕐 Lunch & dinner

La Caprichosa (££)
Harbourside pizzeria with
pasta, meat and fish dishes
and a special children's
menu. Fish soup a speciality.
✉ Cales Fonts 44 ☎ 36 61 58
🕐 Lunch & dinner

Lalola (££)
Popular pizzeria at the
water's edge with a
sandwich bar attached.
✉ Cales Fonts 28 ☎ 36 82 66
🕐 Lunch & dinner

Rocamar (££)
Typical Menorcan restaurant
with the emphasis on grilled
local fish.
✉ Carrer Fonduco 16 ☎ 35
14 63 🕐 Lunch & dinner

Ses Torrades (££)
Just above the fish
restaurants, a meat-lover's
paradise; specialities include
pig's trotters with snails.
Another surprise is a
vegetarian *paella*.
✉ Carrer Ruiz y Pablo 97
☎ 35 49 50 🕐 Lunch &
dinner

Siroco (££)
Fresh fish served simply and
well in a converted cave
beside the harbour. Good-
value *menú del día* with a
separate children's menu.
✉ Cales Fonts 39 ☎ 36 79 65
🕐 All day

Wine
Most wines on offer in
restaurants are imported
from mainland Spain. The
best red wines come from
Rioja, made from the
tempranillo grape and
aged in oak – those
labelled *crianza* are aged
for at least a year, *reserva*
for two, *gran reserva* for
three. Penedés red and
white wines from
Catalunya are good value,
as is *Cava*, Spanish
sparkling wine, which
comes from the same
area.

Caldereta de Langosta

This thick lobster casserole, cooked with onions, tomato, garlic and parsley and served in an earthenware bowl, is the classic seafood dish of Menorca. It comes with thin slices of crispy bread to dip into the soup and a set of tools for tackling the lobster. The best place to eat *caldereta* is at Fornells, where each restaurant has its own recipe. It costs at least 5,000 pesetas per person; a cheaper alternative is *caldereta de mariscos* or *caldereta de peix*, with fish or seafood instead of lobster.

Es Mercadal

Ca'n Aguedet (££)

Considered one of the best restaurants on the island for both traditional and inventive Menorcan cuisine. Booking advised in summer and at weekends.

✉ **Carrer Lepanto 23** ☎ **37 53 91** ⏰ **Lunch & dinner**

Ca'n Olga (££)

Genuine Menorcan cooking in an intimate town house with a vine-covered garden terrace. Booking advised.

✉ **Pont Na Macarrana** ☎ **37 54 59** ⏰ **Dinner Wed–Mon, Sun lunch**

Els Arcs (££)

Spanish and Menorcan cuisine on a garden terrace.

✉ **Carretera Maó–Ciutadella** ☎ **37 55 38** ⏰ **Lunch & dinner**

Jeni (££)

Classic Menorcan dishes, plus a separate children's menu.

✉ **Carrer Mirada del Toro 81** ☎ **37 50 59** ⏰ **Lunch & dinner**

Molí des Recó (££)

An old windmill at the top of the main street. In summer meals are served on a pretty terrace.

✉ **Carrer Vicario Fuxà 53** ☎ **37 53 92** ⏰ **Lunch & dinner**

Es Migjorn Gran

Ca Na Pilar (££)

Imaginative Mediterranean cooking with a pretty garden terrace.

✉ **Carretera Es Mercadal–Es Migjorn** ☎ **37 02 12** ⏰ **Lunch & dinner. Closed Wed**

58 S'Engolidor (££)

Fresh Menorcan cooking in an 18th-century town house with a terrace overlooking a gorge. Booking essential.

✉ **Carrer Major 3** ☎ **37 01 93** ⏰ **Dinner only. Closed Mon**

Ferreries

El Gallo (££)

Charcoal grills a speciality in this 200-year-old farmhouse.

✉ **Carretera Cala Santa Galdana** ☎ **37 30 39** ⏰ **Lunch & dinner. Closed Mon**

Liorna (££)

Arty pizzeria and restaurant; emphasis on modern Catalonian and Italian cuisine.

✉ **Carrer Econom Florit 9** ☎ **37 39 12** ⏰ **Lunch Sat–Sun, dinner Fri–Sun**

Mesón Galicia (££)

Numerous fish specialities and *tapas* from Galicia, in northwest Spain.

✉ **Carrer Maó 17** ☎ **37 38 83** ⏰ **Lunch & dinner**

Fornells

Ca'n Miquel (££)

Small restaurant on the waterfront promenade; speciality rice and fish dishes, including the local spiny lobster.

✉ **Passeig Marítim** ☎ **37 66 23** ⏰ **Lunch & dinner**

Club Náutico (£££)

Lobster delivered to your yacht – at a price.

✉ **Urbanización Ses Salines** ☎ **37 66 03** ⏰ **Mon–Sat, all day in summer**

Es Cranc (£££)

Top-quality local seafood; hidden away in the town so more popular with locals than tourists.

✉ **Carrer Escoles 31** ☎ **37 64 42** ⏰ **Lunch & dinner**

Es Passeig Marítim (££)

Probably the best value of the waterfront restaurants –

pizzas to a gourmet menu featuring octopus, mussels and lobster.

✉ **Passeig Marítim** ☎ 37 63 12 ◷ Lunch & dinner. Closed Sun dinner

Es Pla (£££)

Where King Juan Carlos comes to eat *caldereta de langosta* – there is little point in coming here if you're going to order anything else. Expect to pay at least 8,000 pesetas.

✉ **Passeig des Pla** ☎ 37 66 55 ◷ Lunch & dinner

S'Ancora (££)

Very popular with the expatriate community. Several set menus at different prices.

✉ **Carrer Rosari 23** ☎ 37 66 20 ◷ Lunch & dinner

Ses Salines (££)

Fresh fish and seafood, or sandwiches and pizzas, on a terrace overlooking the bay.

✉ **Urbanización Ses Salines** ☎ 37 66 03 ◷ Lunch & dinner

Punta Prima
Son Ganxo (££)

Long-established restaurant with seafood specialities, home-made desserts and a good-value set menu.

✉ **Carretera Punta Prima–Biniancolla** ☎ 15 16 59 ◷ Lunch & dinner

Sant Climent
Casino San Clemente (££)

Standard international menu in Menorca's oldest and most popular jazz venue.

✉ **Carrer Sant Jaume 2** ☎ 15 34 18 ◷ Lunch & dinner. Closed Wed, jazz on Tue & Thu

Sant Lluís
Ca'n Micky (£)

'Micky's house', beside the football ground, serves

burgers, pizzas, fish and chips, curry and Chinese food.

✉ **Carrer Pedro Tudurí 59** ☎ 15 15 20 ◷ Lunch & dinner. Closed Mon

El Picadero (££)

British-run carvery and barbecue; very popular with local expats.

✉ **Carretera Maó–Sant Lluís** ☎ 36 32 68 ◷ Lunch & dinner

La Rueda (££)

Right in the centre of town; a wide selection of *tapas* in the downstairs bar, a restaurant serving Menorcan specialities upstairs.

✉ **Carrer Sant Lluís 30** ☎ 15 03 49 ◷ Lunch & dinner. Closed Tue

Pan y Vino (££)

British-run restaurant in a charming rural house. Imaginative dishes, plus home-made breads, local cheeses and a wide-ranging wine list.

✉ **Torret 52** ☎ 15 03 22 ◷ Dinner only

Sa Parareta (££)

A country house with a log fire in winter and a garden terrace – with aviary – in summer. Balti curry nights on Mondays, Spanish music and dancing on Wednesdays, fish and chips on Fridays; Sunday roasts.

✉ **Biniburdellet 75** ☎ 15 03 53 ◷ Lunch & dinner. Closed Tue

Sant Tomàs
Riera (££)

Steaks, lobster, pizzas and a children's menu on a shady terrace.

✉ **Urbanización Santo Tomás** ☎ 37 03 96 ◷ Lunch & dinner

Coffee

Most people drink *café solo* after a meal – short, strong and black, like an espresso. If you want your coffee with milk, ask for *café con leche; cortado* is a *café solo* with an extra dash of hot water. The waiter may bring you a glass of brandy or liqueur on the house; ask for a *carajillo* and your coffee will come with brandy already added.

Maó & Ciutadella

Prices

Prices are for a double room, excluding breakfast and VAT:

£ = under 10,000 ptas
££ = 10,000–20,000 ptas
£££ = over 20,000 ptas

These prices will be much lower if you book as part of a package holiday. Most hotels in the resorts are block-booked by tour operators and it is through them that you will get the cheapest deals.

Maó

Capri (££)

Modern, comfortable, three-star hotel close to Plaça de S'Esplanada.

✉ **Carrer Sant Esteve 8**
☎ **36 14 00** 🕐 **All year**

Mirador des Port (££)

Three-star hotel with swimming pool and sea views, 10 minutes' walk from the city centre.

✉ **Carrer Dalt Vilanova 1**
☎ **36 00 16** 🕐 **All year**

Noa (£)

Simple two-star *hostal* on the edge of the city centre.

✉ **Es Cós de Gràcia 157**
☎ **36 12 00** 🕐 **All year**

Orsi (£)

Small, old-fashioned *hostal* in the city centre – the English owner rents out bikes for exploring the city.

✉ **Carrer Infanta 19** ☎ **36 47 51** 🕐 **Feb–Nov**

Port Mahón (£££)

Definitely the best hotel in the capital, in an imposing colonial-style building overlooking the port. Fabulous gardens and a swimming pool.

✉ **Avinguda Fort de l'Eau 13**
☎ **36 26 00** 🕐 **All year**

Ciutadella

Alfonso III (£)

Modern one-star hotel on the edge of the old city.

✉ **Camí de Maó 53** ☎ **38 01 50** 🕐 **All year**

Ciutadella (£)

Modest two-star *hostal* in an old terraced house five minutes' walk from the Plaça des Born.

✉ **Carrer Sant Eloi 10** ☎ **38 34 62** 🕐 **All year**

Esmeralda (££)

Typical 1960s seaside hotel, beside the Passeig Marítim. Most rooms have sea-facing balconies. Swimming pool, tennis courts and a children's play area.

✉ **Camí de Sant Nicolau 171**
☎ **38 02 50** 🕐 **Apr–Oct**

Madrid (£)

One-star hotel with a restaurant, swimming pool and garden, convenient for both the city centre and the sea.

✉ **Carrer Madrid 60** ☎ **38 03 28** 🕐 **May–Oct**

Mar Blava (£)

Two-star *hostal* overlooking the beach at Cala des Degollador.

✉ **Urbanización Son Oleo**
☎ **38 00 16** 🕐 **Apr–Oct**

Menurka (£)

Comfortable two-star *hostal* in the town centre.

✉ **Carrer Fred 6** ☎ **38 14 15**
🕐 **All year**

Oasis (£)

Small, modest *hostal* near ring road with nine rooms around a central courtyard.

✉ **Carrer Sant Isidre 33**
☎ **38 21 97** 🕐 **All year**

Patricia (££)

The best hotel in Ciutadella, popular with business people. A swimming pool, and mini-bars in every room.

✉ **Camí de Sant Nicolau 90**
☎ **38 55 11** 🕐 **Mar–Nov**

Playa Grande (££)

Small, modern hotel beside the beach at Cala des Degollador, with balconies overlooking the start of the Passeig Marítim.

✉ **Carrer Bisbe Juano 2**
☎ **38 24 45** 🕐 **All year**

Around the Island

Arenal d'en Castell

Aguamarina (££)
Three-star hotel above the beach. Disabled access.
✉ **Arenal d'en Castell**
☎ **37 98 17** ⏰ Apr–Oct

Castell Playa (££)
Another hotel overlooking the bay.
✉ **Arenal d'en Castell**
☎ **37 98 88** ⏰ May–Oct

Binibeca Vell

Binivell Park (££)
Houses and apartments for rent in this 'Mediterranean fishing village'.
✉ **Urbanización Binibeca Vell**
☎ **15 06 12** ⏰ Apr–Oct

Cala Blanca

Cala Blanca (££)
Large three-star hotel set in pine woods above the beach, with wheelchair access.
✉ **Urbanización Cala Blanca**
☎ **38 04 50** ⏰ May–Oct

Mediterrani (££)
Big modern three-star hotel close to the beach.
✉ **Urbanización Cala Blanca**
☎ **38 42 03** ⏰ May–Oct

Sagitario Playa (££)
One of the few beach hotels to stay open in winter. Tennis courts and disabled access.
✉ **Avinguda de la Platja 4**
☎ **38 28 77** ⏰ All year

Cala d'Alcaufar

S'Algar (££)
Modern three-star hotel with impressive facilities; most of the rooms have sea views.
✉ **Urbanización S'Algar**
☎ **15 17 00** ⏰ Apr–Oct

San Luis (££)
Large three-star hotel overlooking the sea, with tennis and mini-golf.
✉ **Urbanización S'Algar**
☎ **15 17 50** ⏰ May–Oct

Xuroy (££)
Charmingly old-fashioned two-star *hostal* with its own landing stage right beside the beach at Cala d'Alcaufar.
✉ **Cala d'Alcaufar** ☎ **15 18 20** ⏰ May–Oct

Cala En Blanes

Almirante Farragut (££)
This massive hotel (880 beds) totally dominates the small cove of Cala En Forcat.
✉ **Cala En Forcat** ☎ **38 28 00**
⏰ May–Oct

Cala'n Blanes (££)
Three-star hotel by the beach, with tennis courts and a swimming pool.
✉ **Urbanización Cala En Blanes** ☎ **38 24 97**
⏰ May–Oct

Los Delfines (££)
Two-star hotel at the heart of the Los Delfines tourist complex.
✉ **Urbanización Los Delfines**
☎ **38 24 50** ⏰ May–Oct

Cala En Bosc

Cala'n Bosch (££)
Large hotel with rooms overlooking the sea and all the usual facilities.
✉ **Urbanización Cala En Bosc**
☎ **38 06 00** ⏰ May–Oct

Menorca Star (££)
Three-star 'aparthotel' overlooking the yacht marina.
✉ **Carrer des Port** ☎ **38 58 85** ⏰ May–Oct

Sol Club Falcó (££)
Huge village-style hotel with a full range of facilities.
✉ **Urbanización Son Xoriguer**
☎ **38 46 23** ⏰ May–Oct

Hotels and *Hostals*

All tourist accommodation in Spain is strictly classified and graded by the government. Hotels are graded from one to five stars according to facilities; *hostals*, with fewer facilities but often just as comfortable, are graded from one to three. At levels below three stars you may have to share a bathroom. Most hotels around the coast are closed throughout the winter; *hostals*, and hotels in the main towns, tend to stay open all year.

Package Holidays
The cheapest accommodation in Menorca is available through tour operators and high-street travel agents, booked as part of a package deal with flights and perhaps car hire. As well as having access to cheaper rates at most hotels, many travel agents offer self-catering accommodation and 'agrotourism' holidays, staying in restored farmhouses and on country estates.

Cala En Porter
Aquarium (££)
Modern three-star hotel, with swimming pool and garden, right beside the beach.
✉ **Urbanización Cala En Porter** ☎ **37 70 77** 🕐 **May–Oct**

Playa Azul (££)
One-star hotel with its own swimming pool and play area, facing directly on to the beach.
✉ **Passeig Marítim** ☎ **37 74 21** 🕐 **May–Oct**

Cala Santa Galdana
Audax (£££)
Luxury four-star beach hotel with a rooftop pool and sea-facing balconies.
✉ **Cala Santa Galdana** ☎ **37 31 25** 🕐 **Mar–Oct**

Cala Galdana (££)
Comfortable three-star hotel, behind the beach near the mouth of the Algendar gorge; pool, sauna and children's playground.
✉ **Cala Santa Galdana** ☎ **37 30 00** 🕐 **Apr–Oct**

Sol Gavilanes (££)
Enormous cliff-top hotel towering over the bay with steps leading down to the beach.
✉ **Cala Santa Galdana** ☎ **37 31 75** 🕐 **Apr–Oct**

Es Castell
Almirante (££)
Stylish hotel with antique furniture and paintings and views over Maó harbour.
✉ **Carretera Maó–Es Castell** ☎ **36 27 00** 🕐 **May–Oct**

Agamenón (££)
Three-star hotel by the harbour with its own landing stage.
✉ **Paratge Fontanilles 18** ☎ **36 21 50** 🕐 **Apr–Oct**

Hamilton (££)
Large, old-fashioned hotel in a quiet, central location, with swimming pool, gym and harbour views.
✉ **Passeig Santa Agueda 6** ☎ **36 20 50** 🕐 **All year**

Rey Carlos III (££)
Large three-star hotel with swimming pool and garden overlooking the small harbour at Cala Corb.
✉ **Miranda de Cala Corb** ☎ **36 31 00** 🕐 **May–Oct**

Sol del Este Mar (££)
Modern hotel with swimming pool and children's playground.
✉ **Urbanización Sol del Este** ☎ **36 80 10** 🕐 **All year**

Toni (£)
A simple one-star *hostal* close to the main square.
✉ **Carrer Castillo 3** ☎ **36 59 99** 🕐 **All year**

Es Mercadal
Jeni (£)
Simple but pleasant one-star *hostal* with a good Menorcan restaurant and a rooftop pool.
✉ **Carrer Mirada del Toro 81** ☎ **37 50 59** 🕐 **All year**

Es Migjorn Gran
58 S'Engolidor (££)
Just four rooms in a family-run inn overlooking a gorge. The restaurant downstairs is one of the most celebrated in Menorca.
✉ **Carrer Major 3** ☎ **37 01 93** 🕐 **All year**

Ferreries
Loar (£)
One-star apartment-hotel with its own pool.
✉ **Carrer Reverendo Huguet 2** ☎ **37 41 81** 🕐 **All year**

Fornells

Fornells (£)
Central three-star *hostal* with just 17 rooms and a swimming pool.
✉ **Carrer Major 17** ☎ **37 66 76** ⏰ **All year**

Port Fornells (£)
Two-star *hostal*, conveniently situated for windsurfing and sailing at Ses Salines.
✉ **Urbanización Ses Salines** ☎ **37 63 73** ⏰ **Apr–Oct**

S'Algaret (£)
Basic old-fashioned *hostal* in the centre of town.
✉ **Plaça S'Algaret 7** ☎ **37 66 74** ⏰ **Mar–Nov**

Punta Prima

Pueblo Menorca (££)
Enormous modern hotel with all the trimmings.
✉ **Punta Prima** ☎ **15 18 50** ⏰ **Apr–Oct**

Xaloc (£)
Small one-star hotel on the beach. Rooms have private bathrooms; facilities include swimming pool, play area and mini-golf.
✉ **Platja Punta Prima** ☎ **15 01 06** ⏰ **May–Oct**

Sant Lluís

Biniali (££)
Nine individual rooms in an old farmhouse with its own swimming pool in the countryside to the southwest of the town.
✉ **Carretera S'Uestrà 50** ☎ **15 17 24** ⏰ **Mar–Oct**

Sant Tomàs

Lord Nelson (££)
Three-star hotel above the beach with both indoor and outdoor pools.
✉ **Urbanización Santo Tomás** ☎ **37 01 25** ⏰ **May–Oct**

Santo Tomás (£££)
Four-star hotel close to the beach, with 85 rooms and a large swimming pool.
✉ **Urbanización Santo Tomás** ☎ **37 00 25** ⏰ **May–Oct**

Victoria Playa (££)
Three-star beach hotel with pool, play area and wheelchair access.
✉ **Platja Sant Tomàs** ☎ **37 02 00** ⏰ **May–Oct**

Son Bou

Las Marismas (£££)
Luxury four-star apartment-hotel in the resort of Sant Jaume Mediterrani.
✉ **Urbanización Torre Solí** ☎ **37 80 40** ⏰ **All year**

Sol Milanos (££)
One of the pair of concrete monstrosities which dominate the east end of the beach. The rooms have sea-facing balconies and the hotels share facilities.
✉ **Platja Son Bou** ☎ **37 11 75** ⏰ **May–Oct**

Sol Pinguinos (££)
The matching partner of Sol Milanos (see above).
✉ **Platja Son Bou** ☎ **37 10 75** ⏰ **May–Oct**

Son Valentín Menorca (££)
Four-star 'aparthotel' in pine woods above the sea with rooms specially adapted for disabled visitors.
✉ **Urbanización Torre Solí Nou** ☎ **37 27 48** ⏰ **May–Oct**

Son Parc

Sol Parc (££)
Two-star apartment hotel at the heart of a tourist village built around Menorca's only golf course.
✉ **Urbanización Son Parc** ☎ **18 81 51** ⏰ **May–Oct**

Camping
Menorca has two official campsites, at Son Bou (☎ 37 27 27) and S'Atalaia (☎ 37 30 95), 4km from Ferreries on the road to Cala Santa Galdana. Both are open throughout the year. Unofficial camping is forbidden on beaches, within 1km of a town or 50m of a road. You may camp on farmland with the owner's consent, but never light fires.

Food & Drink

Markets
The two main food markets, in the Carmelite cloisters in Maó and Plaça Libertat in Ciutadella, are open every morning from Monday to Saturday. Most towns in Menorca also have a weekly market, with clothes and craft stalls set up around the main square. Market days are:

Maó – Tue, Sat
Ciutadella – Fri, Sat
Alaior – Thu
Es Castell – Mon, Wed
Es Migjorn Gran – Wed
Ferreries – Tue, Fri

Maó
Ca'n Tiago
As well as local produce, this delicatessen sells cheeses, hams and wine imported from England, France and Spain.
✉ **Carrer Bonaire 26**
☎ **35 23 18**

Es Forn
Old-fashioned bakery with wood-fired ovens on display.
✉ **Carrer La Lluna 28**

Piero's
This delicatessen in the heart of town is a good place to buy Mahón cheese and local liqueurs.
✉ **Carrer Ses Moreres 40**
☎ **36 98 19**

Vallès
Arty pastries and chocolate on Maó's upmarket shopping street.
✉ **Carrer Hannover 19**
☎ **36 34 88**

Xoriguer
Waterfront distillery producing gin and gin-based liqueurs (► 37).
✉ **Moll de Ponent 93**
☎ **36 21 97**

Xoriguer
The distillery also has a shop in the centre of town, with a good range of Spanish wines as well as local gin.
✉ **Plaça del Carme 16** ☎ **36 26 11**

Ciutadella
Diaz
A clock tells you what time the fresh bread will come out of the oven; they also sell ensaimadas from their factory on the edge of town.
✉ **Carrer Santa Clara 19 and**

Poligon Industrial ☎ **48 17 89 and 38 06 50**

El Diamante
Chocolate creations in remarkable designs.
✉ **Carrer JM Quadrado 41 (Ses Voltes)** ☎ **38 09 40**

Miguel Bagur
Pastry shop specialising in boxed ensaimadas and home-made biscuits.
✉ **Carrer JM Quadrado 8 (Ses Voltes)** ☎ **38 06 40**

Ses Industries
Wines, liqueurs, cheese in olive oil plus shelves full of kitsch souvenirs in this Aladdin's cave near the cathedral.
✉ **Carrer Santa Clara 7**
☎ **38 28 82**

Alaior
Coinga
The leading producer of Mahón cheese; the factory shop sells several varieties, from young to very mature.
✉ **Carrer Es Mercadal 8**
☎ **37 12 27**

Es Mercadal
Ca'n Pons
Es Mercadal is known for its almond macaroons, and this is one of the best places to buy them.
✉ **Carrer Nou 13** ☎ **37 50 74**

Ca's Sucrer
Famous for its Villalonga pastries, biscuits and sweets.
✉ **Plaça Constitució 11**

Ferreries
Los Claveles
Specialist bakery producing Menorcan biscuits and pastries.
✉ **Avinguda Verge del Monte Toro 4** ☎ **37 31 28**

Arts, Books & Gifts

Art and Antiques

Maó
Lora
Francesc Lora makes the most celebrated pottery in Menorca at this workshop on the waterfront.
✉ **Moll de Ponent 36** ☎ **35 03 03**

Ciutadella
Huit
Antiques, jewellery and regional Spanish pottery beside the harbour.
✉ **Carrer Marina 73** ☎ **48 27 47**

Loren
High-quality gifts, pottery and glassware.
✉ **Avinguda Conqueridor 97** ☎ **48 21 08**

Es Migjorn Gran
Galeria Migjorn Gran
Watercolours by British artist Graham Byfield, who lives in the village, and by other local artists.
✉ **Carrer Sant Llorenc 12** ☎ **37 03 64**

Books

Maó
Catolica
The best selection of books in Maó, including books on Menorca in English and German.
✉ **Carrer Hannover 15** ☎ **36 35 43**

English Language Library
English books and cards, and copies of the local English-language magazine *Roqueta*.
✉ **Carrer Vassallo 48** ☎ **36 27 01** 🕐 **Mon–Sat 9–1. Closed Sun & Fiestas**

Gifts

Ferreries
Castillo Menorca
The shops in this giant mock castle sell everything Spanish and Menorcan, from Lladró porcelain and Majórica pearls to shoes, leather bags, costume jewellery and highly forgettable souvenirs.
✉ **Carretera Maó–Ciutadella, 35km** ☎ **38 04 24**

New Age/ Alternative

Maó
Body Shop
Cruelty-free cosmetics at the local branch of this well-known international chain.
✉ **Carrer Nou 28** ☎ **35 30 90**

Narayana
A wide range of unusual gifts, including ethnic clothes and jewellery.
✉ **S'Arraval 26**

Ciutadella
Natura
Environment-friendly artefacts – candles, wood, clothes.
✉ **Camí de Maó 3** ☎ **48 20 56**

Raices
Ethnic clothes, jewellery and bright interior designs – go in here just to see the mobiles and listen to the wind chimes.
✉ **Carrer Sant Onofre 8** ☎ **38 56 64**

Samatha
New Age bookshop with candles and incense, hidden among the boutiques on an elegant shopping street.
✉ **Carrer Seminari 22** ☎ **38 41 91**

Opening Hours
Most shops are open from around 10–1:30 and 5–8 Monday to Friday, and on Saturday mornings. Supermarkets and souvenir shops in the resorts will often stay open for longer hours, and the SYP supermarkets in Maó, Ciutadella, Es Mercadal and Ferreries are open from 9–9 Monday to Saturday and 9–1 on Sundays. Many smaller shops, especially in tourist areas, close throughout the winter.

Leather & Jewellery

Shoes

Menorca's shoe industry was founded in the 19th century by Jerónimo Cabrisas, a businessman who emigrated to Cuba and returned to set up an export trade in shoes. At one stage, almost 40 per cent of the population was employed in shoemaking and the industry is still one of the most important on the island. Prices are good if you shop around, and the leather used in the best shoes is wonderfully soft and supple.

Leather

Maó

Complements
As well as leather bags and shoes, this shop has a good range of children's clothes.
✉ **Carrer del Rosari 3** ☎ **36 59 81**

Jaime Mascaro
Maó branch of Menorca's best-known shoe manufacturer; the shop also sells leather jackets and bags.
✉ **Carrer Ses Moreres 29** ☎ **36 95 68**

Looky
Leather and suede waistcoats, handbags and belts, designer T-shirts and locally made shoes.
✉ **Carrer Ses Moreres 43**

Marisa
Elegant boutique on Maó's smartest shopping street, with a fine selection of leather bags.
✉ **Carrer Hannover 7** ☎ **36 27 63**

Mark's
Handbags, belts, suitcases and jackets, sold at two shops in the city centre.
✉ **S'Arravaleta 18 and Carrer Hannover 38** ☎ **36 26 60 and 36 56 25**

Milady
Handbags and ladies' shoes.
✉ **Carrer Nou 37** ☎ **35 36 96**

Musupta
Leather jackets and handbags.
✉ **S'Arravaleta 26** ☎ **36 41 29**

Patricia
Quality shoes and other fashion accessories by a well-known designer.
✉ **Carrer Ses Moreres 31** ☎ **36 91 78**

Riccy
Up-market boutique featuring high-class leather and jewellery.
✉ **Carrer Nou 17**

Vives
Leather shoes and accessories.
✉ **S'Arravaleta 16** ☎ **36 10 14**

Ciutadella

Blau Mari
This fashionable shop in the vaults of the Palau Salord has a wide range of shoes, espadrilles, leather articles and colourful T-shirts.
✉ **Carrer Major del Born 11** ☎ **48 10 95**

Ca Sa Pollaca
This shop has been selling hand-made leather shoes and sandals since 1899; they have a lovely selection of *abarcas* (rubber-soled sandals) for babies and children.
✉ **Carrer JM Quadrado 10 (Ses Voltes)** ☎ **38 22 23**

Jaime Mascaro
A wide selection of men's and women's shoes and other accessories.
✉ **Carrer Verge del Carme 22** ☎ **37 40 27**

Looky
A wide range of shoes and fashion accessories in leather and suede.
✉ **Carrer JM Quadrado 14 (Ses Voltes)** ☎ **38 19 32**

Patricia
Another branch of Patricia's empire, on the road out of

town towards the south coast.

✉ **Carretera Cala Santandría**
☎ 38 50 56

Torres

A large selection of men's and women's shoes, from cheap trainers to high-class leather.

✉ **Camí de Maó 35**
☎ 38 05 00

Es Mercadal

G. Servera

Old-fashioned craftsman producing the local sandals known as *abarcas*, with leather uppers and a sole made out of recycled rubber tyres. Get here early in your holiday and you can have shoes made to measure before you leave.

✉ **Avinguda Metge Camps 3**

Ferreries

Calzados Ferrerias

Ferreries is the centre of shoe production in Menorca and this shop sells the products of one of the two local factories.

✉ **Avinguda Verge del Monte Toro 36** ☎ 15 52 48

Jaime Mascaro

Large factory shop beside the Maó–Ciutadella highway, representing the best-known name in Menorcan shoes.

✉ **Carretera Maó–Ciutadella**
☎ 37 40 27

Jewellery

Maó

Lopez

A wide selection of silver and jewellery, including Majórica pearls from Mallorca.

✉ **Carrer Ses Moreres 58 & 60**
☎ 36 04 78

Nura Moda

Mallorcan pearls and Menorcan costume jewellery at factory prices.

✉ **Poligon Industrial**

Vid

This factory on Maó's industrial estate has a large selction of gold-plated costume jewellery.

✉ **Carrer Capifort 11, Poligon Industrial** ☎ 36 08 50

Ciutadella

Carles

Old-fashioned jewellers' shop in the heart of the old city.

✉ **Carrer Santa Clara 16**
☎ 38 07 34

Joia

Silver earrings and local jewellery, plus a range of arty gifts.

✉ **Plaça des Born 31**

Joies

Smart jewellery shop in the pedestrial part of town.

✉ **Carrer de Maó 6**

Joyería Anglada

Jewellery, silver, gold and Majórica pearls under the arches in Ses Voltes.

✉ **Carrer JM Quadrado 23 (Ses Voltes)** ☎ 38 15 48

Joyería Delfin

Costume jewellery plus art and antiques in one of Ciutadella's smartest shopping streets.

✉ **Carrer Seminari 16** ☎ 38 08 88

Vid

A branch of the factory in Maó which produces much of Menorca's costume jewellery.

✉ **Carrer Major del Born 9**

Costume Jewellery

One of Menorca's leading industries is the manufacture of costume jewellery, using common metals which are coated with silver or gold and finished with imitation stones. The effect is to create something extravagant, yet without the expense of precious metal or gems. Most of the costume jewellery produced in Menorca is exported to South America, but there are still bargains to be had – especially at the two annual fairs of costume jewellery, SEBIME, held in Maó's trade fair centre in May and September.

Children's Attractions

Looking After Children

Small children are particularly vulnerable to the sun and need to be protected; apply a high-factor sun block regularly, especially after swimming. If you need a child seat in your hire car, make sure to book it in advance and check it carefully on arrival. The same goes for cots and high-chairs in hotels and apartments. Finally, don't forget to check that your balcony railings are secure.

Menorca is a very child-friendly society. Like other Mediterranean people, the Spanish are known for their love of children and no-one is going to complain if you take your child out to a good restaurant in the evening.

Menorca is ideal for family holidays. A large number of hotels have children's nurseries and baby-sitting services (these are listed in the Where to Stay section) and package-tour operators will lay on children's activities during the day. Every town and beach resort has at least one children's playground, and very often these are found in hotels too. Some hotels also have mini-golf circuits and children's pools. Make sure you ask your hotel or travel agent about these facilities before you go.

Most children are happy enough just being on the beach – and fortunately Menorca has a wealth of child-friendly beaches, with safe, shallow water and Red Cross posts in case of emergency. It is easy to buy beach toys; for bigger thrills, take the children for a ride on a pedal boat or an inflatable banana. Do remember, though, that children are especially vulnerable to dangerous conditions, and never let them go into the sea when the red danger flag is flying.

Children will enjoy the 'road trains' which make a circuit of the resorts at Son Bou, S'Algar and Cala En Bosc in summer. The following is a list of other activities which will particularly appeal to children. All of them only operate during the summer season, usually from May to October.

Animals

Alaior

Ostriches de Menorca

Menorca's only ostrich ranch is open to the public for visits in summer.

✉ **Carretera Alaior–Es Migjorn Gran** ☎ **18 83 46** 🕐 **Tue–Sun 11–2, 4–8**

Picadero Menorca

This ranch on the outskirts of Alaior offers pony rides and rides in a horse and cart.

✉ **Carretera Son Bou** 🚌 **Buses from Maó and Alaior in summer**

Cala d'Alcaufar

Picadero Es Boeret

Riding school offering pony rides and displays of horsemanship.

✉ **Urbanización S'Algar** ☎ **15 10 49** 🚌 **Buses from Maó in summer**

Ferreries

Club Escola Menorquina

The equestrian show here features carriage rides, dressage displays and performances of prancing and rearing similar to that which you see in traditional Menorcan *festas*. Children get the chance to go for a donkey ride during the interval.

✉ **Carretera Ferreries–Cala Santa Galdana, km0.5** ☎ **37 34 97** 🕐 **Jun–Sep, Wed & Sun 8PM**

Son Parc

Donkey Safari Park

Mule and donkey rides through the woods at this farm on the road from Maó to Fornells.

✉ **Carretera Maó–Fornells, km15** ☎ **37 83 42** 🕐 **Daily in summer**

Adventure

Cala Blanca
Los Toboganes
Basically a pizza restaurant overlooking the beach, but children will enjoy trying out the crazy golf course, toboggan slope and water-slide while their parents eat.
✉ **Urbanización Cala Blanca**
☎ **38 51 68**

Cala Santa Galdana
Tobogán
Like its cousin at Cala Blanca (see above), this bar-pizzeria features mini-golf, a toboggan slope and a thrilling water-slide.
✉ **Cala Santa Galdana**

Ferreries
Costa Nova
Teenagers can take a ride in a go-kart while the others browse in the Castillo Menorca shopping complex.
✉ **Carretera Maó–Ciutadella, km35** ☎ **38 04 24** ⏰ **10–8 daily**

Son Bou
Club San Jaime
This is the top children's attraction on the island – a wealth of activities to keep little ones amused, including a swimming pool, a water-chute and a remarkable interlocking wooden maze which can be rearranged to get harder as you go along. There are several bars and restaurants to keep the grown-ups happy. The whole complex is arranged around a series of attractively landscaped gardens with views down over the marshes and out to sea.
✉ **Sant Jaume Mediterrani**
☎ **37 27 87** ⏰ **Apr–Oct, 10–10 daily**

Beaches
The following beaches are particularly suitable for children. All have shallow water, plenty of sand, and are easily reached by car. You can rent pedaloes at all of these beaches in summer; some of the larger ones (such as Cala Santa Galdana and Son Parc) also have canoes and motor boats for hire.

Arenal d'en Castell
Binibeca
Cala Blanca
Cala d'Alcaufar
Cala En Porter
Cala Santa Galdana
Cala Santandría
Es Grau
Son Bou
Son Parc

Boat Trips
Children always enjoy the thrill of the open water and there are numerous boat excursions around the Menorcan coast in summer. Services vary throughout the season so it is best to ask at your hotel or look out for notices on the quayside. A popular option is a full-day trip to a cove that cannot be reached by road; the price often includes lunch, usually a *paella* cooked on the beach. Another option is to charter your own yacht or motor boat and simply set off to explore.

Popular boat trips include:
Cala En Bosc to Arenal de Son Saura and Cala En Turqueta.
Cala Santa Galdana to Cala Trebalúger.
Ciutadella to Arenal de Son Saura and Cala En Turqueta.
Es Grau to Illa d'en Colom.
Port d'Addaia to Fornells.

Family Outings
As well as the attractions listed here, children will enjoy the trotting races at Maó and Ciutadella (► 113), the Molí de Dalt windmill at Sant Lluís (► 83) and the boat tours of Maó harbour (► 23).

109

Art Galleries, Cinemas & Theatres

What's On?

To find out what's on while you're staying, ask at your hotel or the tourist offices in Maó and Ciutadella, or check the listings in the daily paper *Menorca* and the English-language monthly *Roqueta*. In Ciutadella you can also look at the billboards which are displayed in Ses Voltes. Everything starts late – plays at around 9PM, films at 10, and music at any time up to midnight.

Art Galleries

Maó

Sala de Cultura Carrer Nou
A gallery in the heart of the pedestrian shopping quarter hosting temporary exhibitions of modern art.
✉ **Carrer Nou 25**

Sala de Cultura Sa Nostra
Art exhibitions in the former convent of Sant Antoni.
✉ **S'Arraval 32** ☎ **36 68 54**

Ciutadella

Centre de Cultura Sa Nostra
Exhibition rooms and educational activities.
✉ **Carrer Santa Clara 9** ☎ **48 06 86** 🕐 **Mon–Fri 10–12, 6:30–8:30; Sat 7–9**

Església del Roser
Occasional art exhibitions are held inside this restored 17th-century baroque church.
✉ **Carrer del Roser**

Museu del Pintor Torrent
Collection of works by José Torrent (► 41).
✉ **Carrer Rafel 11** 🕐 **11–1, 7:30–9:30 daily in summer; Fri/Sat 7–9PM and Sat 11–1 in winter**

Es Migjorn Gran

Galeria Migjorn Gran
Exhibitions of work by the British watercolour artist Graham Byfield and other local artists.
✉ **Carrer Sant Llorenc 12** ☎ **37 03 64** 🕐 **Apr–Dec, Tue–Sat 10–1, 6–9**

Cinemas

Maó

Cine Alcazar
✉ **Carrer Santa Ana 27** ☎ **36 34 06**

Cine Salón Victoria
Dilapidated picture-house showing films at weekends.
✉ **Carrer Sant Roc 24** ☎ **36 39 10**

Teatre Principal
Maó's opera house and theatre also shows films.
✉ **Costa d'en Deià 46** ☎ **36 98 00 (town hall)**

Ciutadella

Cinema des Born
Films are frequently shown in the city's theatre.
✉ **Plaça des Born** ☎ **38 01 76**

Cinema OAR
The city's main cinema, with the latest Spanish films and international blockbusters dubbed into Spanish.
✉ **Avinguda Capita Negrete 1** ☎ **38 05 97**

Alaior

Centro Cultural Alaior
The Cine Club in Alaior's cultural centre shows occasional films on Tuesdays and at weekends.
✉ **Carrer Nou**

Theatres

Maó

Teatre Principal
An elegant opera house with films, plays and a spring opera season in March and April. For the best views book a seat in one of the 80 boxes.
✉ **Costa d'en Deià 46** ☎ **36 98 00 (town hall)**

Ciutadella

Teatre Municipal des Born
The city's theatre in a 19th-century neo-classical building in a corner of the Born.
✉ **Plaça des Born** ☎ **38 01 76**

Music & Nightlife

Most of the late-night action in summer takes place in and around the big tourist resorts, where foreign-owned bars and pubs offer familiar accents and familiar beer. These come and go every season and the only advice is to follow your nose. To meet locals as well as tourists, head for some of these more established bars in the main towns.

Bars and Clubs

Maó
Akelarre
This waterfront bar is slightly older than some of the others, attracting a sophisticated yachting crowd with its laid-back music and 'maritime cocktails'.
✉ **Moll de Ponent 42** ☎ **36 85 20**

Café Baixamar
Late-night meeting place of the young and trendy, on the waterfront.
✉ **Moll de Ponent 17**

Jazz Cava
Nightclub with live music from 11PM at weekends – jazz on Thursday, ballroom dancing Friday and Saturday.
✉ **Plaça Princep 12** ☎ **35 35 21**

Nashville
'Beer and soundhouse' on the seafront with loud music and German and American food.
✉ **Moll de Llevant 147** ☎ **36 79 56** ⏰ **Daily 9AM–3AM**

Salsa
Trendy nightspot with cool Latin sounds, close to the ferry port.
✉ **Moll de Ponent 29**

Ciutadella
Asere
Salsa club with Cuban music and cocktails – go late.
✉ **Carrer Corniola 23** ☎ **38 38 52**

El Mosquito
Popular *club de salsa* .
✉ **Carrer Sa Muradeta 16**
⏰ **From 11PM at weekends**

Sa Xarxa
Loud rock music for a young, late-night crowd; in the heart of the old city.
✉ **Carrer Sant Sebastià 2**

Es Castell
Es Cau
Bring your own instruments to this lively music bar, situated by the harbour inside a cave. The emphasis is on folk music, including traditional fishermen's songs.
✉ **Cala Corb**

Piano Bar
Cool, late-night cocktail bar.
✉ **Carrer Sant Ignasi II**
☎ **36 40 22** ⏰ **From 10:30PM daily**

Sant Climent
Casino San Clemente
Menorca's oldest jazz venue, with a large expat following. Sessions are held throughout the summer and visitors are encouraged to join in.
✉ **Carrer Sant Jaume 2**
☎ **15 34 18** ⏰ **Jazz nights on Tue & Thu, Apr–Oct. Closed Wed**

Sant Lluís
Hipódromo
Music every Saturday night in summer at Maó's municipal racecourse.
✉ **Carretera Maó–Sant Lluís**
☎ **36 57 30**

Classical Music Festivals
As well as Maó's spring opera season, there are international festivals of young musicians each summer in Maó (☎ 36 47 98) and Ciutadella. Organ recitals are held daily from July to September in Maó's Santa Maria church, and a series of Easter concerts takes place in the main churches in Maó, Ciutadella, Alaior, Es Mercadal and Ferreries. Throughout August there are recitals every Thursday evening in the church of Sant Antoni in Fornells.

Discos

Cova d'en Xoroi

This bar and disco is set inside a natural cave, high in the cliff-face above the sea. There are numerous stairways and rock platforms, and a dance floor precariously overlooking the sea. Open during the day for drinks, it turns into a disco at night and gets busy after midnight. There is an interesting Arabic legend attached to the cave (➤ 58).

By their very nature, discos come and go – what's in this year will already be *passé* by next, and changes of name and image are essential to keep the punters rolling in. Most of the larger resorts will have a disco of one kind or another, sometimes based in a hotel nightclub, and the only thing to do is to ask around or listen out for the disco beat. These are a few of the island's more established discos, or *salas de fiestas* ('party halls'). Most are open nightly throughout the peak tourist season, but only at weekends – if at all – in winter. They mostly get busy around midnight.

Maó
Si

Cool late-night spot with a name which means 'yes'. Or should that be yes, yes, yes…

✉ **Carrer Verge de Gràcia 16**
☎ **36 13 62**

Ciutadella
Lateral

The old warehouses around the Pla de Sant Joan, the open space behind the marina, are home to numerous clubs and discos which get busy around midnight and continue well into the small hours. This is the best-known but others include Solo, L'Herba and Wee Kee Lee. Just choose the music and the décor whcih suits your style – they change from year to year.

✉ **Pla de Sant Joan 9**

Cala En Blanes
Danzas

Disco at the heart of the extensive Los Delfines tourist complex around the bay of Cala En Forcat.

✉ **Urbanización Los Delfines**
☎ **38 30 45**

Cala En Porter
Cova d'en Xoroi

Menorca's most unusual disco (see panel).

✉ **Urbanización Cala En Porter**
☎ **37 72 36**

Sant Lluís
Jaleo

Large, flashy nightclub, formerly known as Pachas.

✉ **Avinguda Sant Lluís** ☎ **15 01 72**

Son Bou
San Jaime

Part of the Club San Jaime complex in the neighbouring resort of Sant Jaume Mediterrani.

✉ **Urbanización Sant Jaume**
☎ **37 27 87**

Street Parties

Large, outdoor street parties featuring discos and live music are a feature of all Menorca's main festivals (➤ 116). During the festival of La Verge del Gràcia, in Maó in September, outdoor concerts are held each evening in various venues including Plaça de S'Esplanada, Plaça Miranda and the harbourside. These are a great way of meeting local people and soaking up the atmosphere of a Menorcan party. For details, check in the local paper or simply ask around at festival time in the local bars.

There are also occasional rock concerts at Maó's sports stadium, Polideportivo Municipal (☎ 36 76 61). Look for details in the local paper.

Spectator & Participatory Sport

Cricket

Sant Lluís
Menorca Cricket Club
The British expatriate community in Menorca keep their national game going, with games against visiting sides from Britain and Spain at weekends in summer.
✉ Urbanización Biniparell

Football

Maó
Estadio Mahonés
Sporting Mahón are hardly one of Spain's big-name teams (most locals prefer to watch Barcelona on television) but if you want to see them in action, they are at home on alternate Sunday afternoons throughout the season.
✉ Avinguda Josep Anselm Clavé ☎ 36 40 79 🕐 Check times of games in the local paper

Golf

Son Parc
Club Son Parc
Menorca's only golf course, a short 9-hole course opened in 1977. Par 70. Tuition is available and you can hire clubs and equipment.
✉ Urbanización Son Parc ☎ 18 88 75 🕐 Daily

Horse-racing

Maó/Sant Lluís
Hipódromo de Maó
Trotting races (see panel) are held here throughout the year, on Saturday evenings in summer and Sunday mornings in winter.
✉ Carretera Maó–Sant Lluís ☎ 36 57 30

Ciutadella/Cala En Blanes
Hipódromo de Ciutadella
Trotting races held on Sundays throughout the year.
✉ Torre del Ram, Cala En Forcat ☎ 38 41 32

Horse Riding

Horse and pony hire and excursions are available from the following centres.

Alaior
Picadero Menorca
✉ Carretera Son Bou ☎ 37 18 52

Cala d'Alcaufar
Picadero Es Boeret
✉ Urbanización S'Algar ☎ 15 10 49

Sant Climent
Picadero Binixica
✉ Carretera Cala En Porter ☎ 15 30 71

Tennis

Many of the larger hotels have tennis courts for their guests, but these clubs are all open to visitors.

Maó
Club de Tenis Mahón
✉ Camino Trepucó 4 ☎ 36 05 76

Alaior
Club de Tenis Alaior
✉ Camí de Talaia ☎ 37 15 89

Cala En Blanes
Club de Tenis Ciutadella
✉ Torre del Ram, Cala En Forcat ☎ 38 20 68

Ferreries
Club de Tenis Ferreries
✉ Carrer Sant Bartomeu ☎ 15 51 27

Trotting
Trotting has been popular in the Balearic Islands for at least 200 years; at one time neighbouring villages used to hold trotting races against each other. The jockey sits in a small cart behind the horse and has to prevent his horse from breaking into a gallop. A handicap system ensures that weaker horses get a head start on the others. The trotting races in Maó and Ciutadella at weekends make a great excuse for a family day out with a picnic – and a few bets on the side.

Watersports

Sailing in Menorca
The calm waters around Menorca are perfect for sailing – there are no tides, few currents and the only real hazard is the *tramuntana* wind. There are long, sheltered bays at Maó, Fornells and Port d'Addaia and smaller inlets at Es Grau and Ciutadella; all of these are suitable for novice sailors but only experienced hands should tackle the open sea. You can charter yachts at any of the nautical clubs.

Sailing

Nautical clubs

Maó
Club Marítimo
✉ Moll de Llevant 287
☎ 36 50 22

Ciutadella
Club Náutico
✉ Camí de Baix ☎ 38 39 18

Es Castell
Club Náutico
✉ Cales Fonts ☎ 36 58 84

Fornells
Club Náutico
✉ Ses Salines ☎ 37 64 00

Port d'Addaia
Club Náutico
✉ Port d'Addaia ☎ 36 32 07

Sailing Schools

The following schools offer tuition in sailing and windsurfing at all levels of ability.

Ciutadella
Surf 'n' Sail Menorca
☎ 908 636 235

Binibeca Vell
Cala Torret
✉ Urbanización Cala Torret
☎ 908 539 955

Fornells
Servinàutic Menorca
✉ Carrer Major 27
☎ 37 66 36

Windsurf Fornells
✉ Carrer Rosari 169
☎ 37 64 00

Punta Prima
Menorca Cruising School
✉ Urbanización Biniancollet
☎ 15 17 38

Repair Facilities

Maó
Pedro's Boat Centre
☎ 36 69 68

Ciutadella
Pedro's Boat Centre
☎ 48 12 29

Scuba Diving

Diving Schools

Maó
Scuba Menorca
✉ Moll de Llevant 4 ☎ 35 13 63

Ciutadella
Sports Massanet
☎ 38 03 49

Binibeca Vell
Cala Torret
✉ Urbanización Cala Torret
☎ 18 85 30

Cala d'Alcaufar
Club S'Algar
✉ Urbanización S'Algar
☎ 15 06 01

Cala En Bosc
Crystal Seas Scuba
✉ Urbanización Cala En Bosc
☎ 38 70 38

Hotel Club Falcó
✉ Urbanización Cala En Bosc
☎ 38 46 23

Sub Menorca
✉ Urbanización Cala En Bosc
☎ 38 71 05

Cala Santa Galdana
Diving Center
✉ Hotel Gavilanes ☎ 908 433 720

Es Castell
Florit Sub
Carrer Gran 83 ☎ 36 52 59

Fornells
Centro de Buceo Fornells
✉ Carrer Verge del Carme 28
☎ 37 66 94

Club Ulmo
✉ Coves Noves ☎ 35 80 98

Servinàutic Menorca
✉ Carrer Major 27 ☎ 37 66 36

Swimming
Most resort hotels have outdoor swimming pools and a few have heated indoor pools as well. Swimming in the sea is generally safe but you should beware of currents at the remoter coves and look out for the safety flag system at those beaches manned by the Red Cross – a red flag warns of danger, a green flag means it is safe to swim. It is generally warm enough to swim in the sea from June to October. A few Menorcan beaches have been awarded the European Union Blue Flag – these are supposed to be safe, clean and well-kept. Blue Flag beaches include those at Arenal d'en Castell, Binibeca, Cala Santa Galdana, Cala Santandría, Es Grau and Son Xoriguer (near Cala En Bosc).

Polideportivo Municipal
Maó's sports stadium includes Menorca's only public indoor pool, open throughout the year.
✉ Polígon Industrial
☎ 36 76 61

Water-skiing
Water-skiing is available on several of the larger beaches in summer, including Arenal d'en Castell, Cala Blanca, Cala Santa Galdana and Son

Bou. You can also water-ski behind your own motorboat, but it is essential to show respect to other sea-users and to stay well away from swimmers and divers. Water-skiing is forbidden in Maó and Ciutadella harbours. The following clubs offer tuition for beginners.

Cala d'Alcaufar
Club S'Algar
✉ Urbanización S'Algar
☎ 15 06 01

Fornells
Servinàutic Menorca
✉ Carrer Major 27 ☎ 37 66 36

Windsurfing
Windsurfing boards and equipment are available for hire at several of the larger resorts; the place to ask is usually at the beach bar. Tuition is sometimes available as well – the sheltered coves and bays around the island create ideal conditions for beginners, particularly in the Bay of Fornells. The sailing schools listed above all provide instruction in windsurfing as well.

Beach Activities
At most of the larger beaches it is possible to rent a range of equipment for fun and games out on the water. Most popular are pedaloes, ideal for gentle family outings. Canoes and kayaks are also widely available. For a real adrenalin rush, you can go out on a jet-ski, or take a banana ride on a giant inflatable banana as it is towed at speed through the water. Wear a life-jacket.

Diving in Menorca
The clear waters in many of Menorca's bays make for excellent diving. Besides the wealth of marine life, there are also numerous caves to explore and shipwrecks to discover off Cala Mesquida, Punta Natí and Son Bou. Diving is expensive – a single dive might cost 5,000 pesetas – and you are required to take out both insurance and membership of the Spanish diving federation. Remember, it can be dangerous to fly less than 24 hours after diving.

What's On When

Festivals in Menorca

Most of Menorca's festivals are Christian in origin, with touches of pagan ritual and a passion for horses introduced by the Arabs. Each town has its own *festa*, in honour of its patron saint – a week of parties, concerts and sporting events culminates in a final weekend of festivities, with horseback processions, music and dancing and a midnight firework display in the main square.

January

Los Reyes Magos (5 Jan): The Three Kings arrive by boat in Maó to deliver Christmas presents to the city's children the next day. Similar events take place across the island.

Sant Antoni Abad (16–17 Jan): Bonfires, dancing and fancy dress parties in Maó, Es Castell and elsewhere on 16 January; on 17 January, following a Mass in Ciutadella cathedral, there is a horseback procession to Plaça Alfons III.

March/April

Setmana Santa (Holy Week): Palm branches are blessed in the island's churches on Palm Sunday and taken home to adorn balconies and front doors. Processions in Maó and Ciutadella on Good Friday.

June

Sant Joan (23–24 Jun): This is the most colourful of all Menorca's festivals, with traditions dating back to the Middle Ages. On the evening of 23 June is a horseback procession around the Plaça des Born in Ciutadella, and on 24 June there are further processions, a Mass in the cathedral, jousting tournaments and finally a firework display in the Born.

July

Festa Patriòtica (9 Jul): A day of festivities in Ciutadella to commemorate the city's resistance against the Turkish attack in 1558.

La Verge del Carme (16 Jul): Processions of fishing boats in Maó, Ciutadella and Fornells in honour of the protector of fishermen.

Sant Martí (3rd weekend): Processions of horses, giants and Carnival figures in Es Mercadal.

Sant Jaume (24–26 Jul): Horseback parades and merriment in Es Castell.

Sant Antoni (4th weekend): Annual festivities in Fornells, including *jaleo* dancing on the waterfront.

August

Sant Cristòfol (early Aug): Es Migjorn Gran's annual festival features a 'blessing of the vehicles' by the parish priest.

Sant Llorenç (Sun after 10 Aug): *Caragols* dancing and prancing in the streets of Alaior.

Sant Climent (3rd weekend): Equestrian fun and games in Sant Climent.

Sant Bartomeu (23–25 Aug): Frolics in Ferreries, with cavalcades, music and dancing.

Sant Lluís (last weekend): Parades, parties and firework displays.

September

La Verge del Gràcia (7–9 Sep): Maó's main festival features cavalcades, street parties, donkey races, firework displays and regattas in the harbour.

December

Nadal (Christmas, 24–25 Dec): Midnight Mass in churches across Menorca.

Practical Matters

TIME DIFFERENCES

GMT	Menorca	Germany	USA (NY)	Netherlands	Rest of Spain
12 noon	→ 1PM	→ 1PM	← 7AM	→ 1PM	→ 1PM

BEFORE YOU GO

WHAT YOU NEED

● Required
○ Suggested
▲ Not required

	UK	Germany	USA	Netherlands	Spain
Passport/National Identity Card	●	●	●	●	▲
Visa	▲	▲	▲	▲	▲
Onward or Return Ticket	○	○	●	○	○
Health Inoculations	▲	▲	▲	▲	▲
Health Documentation (► 123, Health)	●	●	●	●	▲
Travel Insurance	○	○	○	○	○
Driving Licence (national with Spanish translation or International)	●	●	●	●	●
Car Insurance Certificate	●	●	●	●	○
Car Registration Document	●	●	●	●	○

WHEN TO GO

Menorca

High season

Low season

14°C	15°C	17°C	19°C	22°C	26°C	29°C	29°C	27°C	23°C	18°C	15°C
JAN	FEB	MAR	APR	MAY	JUN	JUL	AUG	SEP	OCT	NOV	DEC

Wet　　Cloud　　Sun　　Showers/Sun

TOURIST OFFICES

In the UK
Spanish Tourist Office
22–3 Manchester Square
London W1M 5AP
☎ 0171 486 8077
Fax: 0171 486 8034

In the USA
Tourist Office of Spain
666 Fifth Avenue 35th
New York
NY 10103
☎ 212/265 8822
Fax: 212/265 8864

Tourist Office of Spain
8383 Wilshire Boulevard
Suite 960
Beverly Hills
Cal 90211
☎ 213/658 7188
Fax: 213/658 1061

| POLICE (POLICÍA NACIONAL) 091 |
| FIRE (BOMBEROS) 351011 |
| AMBULANCE (AMBULÀNCIA) 061 |
| RED CROSS (CRUZ ROJA) 361180 |

WHEN YOU ARE THERE

ARRIVING

Spain's national airline, Iberia (☎ 901 333222), has scheduled flights to Menorca from the Spanish mainland and major European and North American cities, but most visitors arrive by charter plane. Ferry services operate from Barcelona and Valencia on the Spanish mainland.

Maó (San Clemente) Airport to town centre	Journey times
5 kilometres	🚇 N/A
	🚌 N/A
	🚗 10 minutes

Maó Ferry Terminal in town centre	Journey times
	🚇 N/A
	🚌 available
	🚗 available

MONEY

Spain's currency is the peseta, issued in notes of 1,000, 2,000, 5,000 and 10,000 pesetas and coins of 5, 10, 25, 50, 100, 200 and 500 pesetas. A one-peseta coin still exists but most bills are rounded down to the nearest 5 pesetas. Traveller's cheques are accepted by most hotels, shops and restaurants in lieu of cash, although the rate of exchange may be less favourable than in banks. Traveller's cheques in pesetas are the most convenient. Banks can be found in most towns in Menorca and handle traveller's cheques, Eurocheques and give advances on credit cards.

TIME

Like the rest of Spain, Menorca is one hour ahead of Greenwich Mean Time (GMT+1), but from late March until late September, summer time (GMT+2) operates.

CUSTOMS

 YES

Goods Obtained Duty Free Inside the EU or Goods Bought Outside the EU (Limits):
Alcohol (over 22° vol): 1L *or*
Alcohol (not over 22° vol): 2L *and* Still table wine: 2L
Cigarettes: 200 *or*
Cigars: 50 *or*
Tobacco: 250gms
Perfume: 50gms
Toilet water: 250ml
Goods Bought Duty and Tax Paid Inside the EU (Guidance Levels):
Alcohol (over 22° vol): 10L *and*
Alcohol (not over 22° vol): 20L *and*
Wine (max 60L sparkling): 90L *and* Beer: 110L
Cigarettes: 800 *and*
Cigars: 200 *and* Tobacco: 1kg
Perfume: no limit
Toilet water: no limit
You must be 17 and over to benefit from the tobacco and alcohol allowances.

 NO

Drugs, firearms, ammunition, offensive weapons, obscene material, unlicensed animals.

CONSULATES

UK
☎ 363373

Germany
☎ 722371

USA
☎ 722660

Netherlands
☎ 716493

WHEN YOU ARE THERE

TOURIST OFFICES

**Menorca Island Council
(Consell Insular de Menorca)**

● Cami Castell 28
07702 – Maó
Menorca
☎ 351515
Fax: 368216

**Tourist Information Centres
(Oficinas d'Informació
Turística)**

● Plaça de S'Esplanada 40
07701 – Maó
Menorca
☎ 363790
Fax: 367415
Open: Mon–Fri, 8AM–3PM
and 5PM–7PM;
Sat, 9AM–2PM

● Plaça de la Catedral
0707760 – Ciutadella
Menorca
☎ 382693
Fax: 382667
Open: Mon–Fri, 8AM–3PM
and 5PM–7PM, (9AM–2PM,
Nov–Apr); Sat, 9:30AM–1PM

● Maó Airport
San Clemente
☎ 157115
Open: May–Oct daily
8:30AM–11PM

Each office can supply you
with a free map of the
island plus information on
accommodation, places to
visit, beaches, buses, ferries,
car rental, etc.

NATIONAL HOLIDAYS

J	F	M	A	M	J	J	A	S	O	N	D
2		(1)	(1)	1(2)	(1)	1	1		1	1	3

1 Jan	New Year's Day
6 Jan	Epiphany
Mar/Apr	Good Friday, Easter Monday
1 May	Labour Day
May/Jun	Corpus Christi
25 Jul	Saint James' Day
15 Aug	Assumption of the Virgin
12 Oct	National Day
1 Nov	All Saints' Day
6 Dec	Constitution Day
8 Dec	Feast of the Immaculate Conception
25 Dec	Christmas Day

Shops, banks and offices close on these days but in
the main resorts many places remain open.

OPENING HOURS

○ Shops	● Churches
● Offices	● Museums
● Banks	● Pharmacies

| 8AM | 9AM | 10AM | NOON | 1PM | 2PM | 4PM | 5PM | 6PM | 7PM |

□ Day   □ Midday
□ Evening

Large department stores, supermarkets and shops in
tourist resorts may open outside these times,
especially in summer. In general, pharmacies, banks
and shops close on Saturday afternoon, though banks
stay open until 4:30PM Monday to Thursday, October
to May, but close Saturday, June to September.

The opening times of museums is just a rough guide;
some are open longer hours in summer while hours
are reduced in winter. Some museums close at
weekends and/or Monday.

DRIVE ON THE RIGHT

TOILETS FREE

PUBLIC TRANSPORT

Inter-Island Flights Iberia operates several flights a day between Mallorca and Menorca (flight time: 30 minutes). There are no direct flights from Menorca to Ibiza (you are routed via Mallorca). Fares are inexpensive but you must book ahead at the height of summer (Iberia domestic flight reservations ☎ 901 333111). For Maó airport information ☎ 360150. (➤ 119, Arriving.)

Buses Menorca has an extensive network of buses (operator: Transportes Menorca, ☎ 360361) linking the main towns of Maó and Ciutadella with most coastal resorts and interior villages, supplemented by moire intermittent local services between smaller towns and between neighbouring resorts. Destinations are marked on the front of the bus. Always check the time of the last bus back.

Inter-island Ferries There are sea services between Menorca and Mallorca. Trasmediterránea (☎ 366050) operates a weekly car ferry between Palma and Maó (6 hours). Also, Flebasa (☎ 480012) runs a twice-daily (mid-April to December) ferry service between Port d'Alcúdia and Ciutadella (3½ hours), and a hydrofoil (no cars) thrice daily from mid-June to mid-September (1 hour).

Urban Transport Only Maó and Ciutadella are large enough to have their own transport systems. In Maó local buses depart from the square across from the tourist office (➤ 120, Tourist Offices), however its narrow, congested streets make exploring on foot a better option. In Ciutadella local buses stop on Plaça S'Esplanada on the west side of the town centre.

CAR RENTAL

The leading international car rental companies have offices at Maó airport and you can book a car in advance (essential in peak periods) either direct or through a travel agent. Local companies offer competitive rates and will usually deliver a car to the airport.

TAXIS

Taxis can be hired at ranks (indicated by a blue square with a 'T'), on the street (by flagging down those with a green light), or at hotels. They are good value within Maó but expensive over long distances. A list of tariffs is displayed at taxi ranks.

DRIVING

There are no motorways. The only main road links Maó and Ciutadella (speed limit: **100kph**)

Speed limit on minor roads: **90kph**

Speed limit on urban roads: **60kph**

Must be worn in front seats at all times and in rear seats where fitted.

Random breath-testing. Limit: 80 micrograms of alcohol in 100ml of breath.

Fuel (*gasolina*) is available in four grades: *Super Plus* (98 octane), *Super* (96 octane) and often unleaded (*sin plomo*), *Mezcla* or *Normal* (90 octane), and *gasoleo* or *gasoil* (diesel). Petrol stations, few and far between, are normally open 6AM–10PM, and closed Sundays, though larger ones (often self service) are open 24 hours. Most take credit cards.

If you break down driving your own car and are a member of an AIT-affiliated motoring club, you can call the Real Automóvil Club de España (☎ 91 593 3333). If the car is hired follow the instructions given in the documentation; most of the international rental firms provide a rescue service.

CENTIMETRES
0 1 2 3 4 5 6 7 8

INCHES
0 1 2 3

PERSONAL SAFETY

The national police force, the Policía Nacional (brown uniforms) keep law and order in urban areas. Some resorts have their own tourist-friendly Policía Turística. If you need a police station ask for *la comisaría*.

To help prevent crime:
- Do not carry more cash than you need.
- Do not leave valuables on the beach or poolside.
- Beware of pickpockets in markets, tourist sights or crowded places.
- Avoid walking alone in dark alleys at night.

Police assistance:
☎ **091**
from any call box

TELEPHONES

A public telephone (*teléfono*) takes 25, 100 and 500-peseta coins. A phonecard (*credifone*) is available from post offices and *tabacos* for 1,000 or 2,000 pesetas.

All telephone numbers in the Balearic Islands have the same code (971), so within Menorca you need dial only the six-figure numbers shown in this guide. To call the operator ☎ 002. For directory enquiries ☎ 003.

International Dialling Codes

From Menorca (Spain) to:	
UK:	07 44
Germany:	07 49
USA:	07 1
Netherlands:	07 31

POST

Post Offices
There are post offices (*correus*) in every town and most villages. They are open as below but some also open in the afternoon and on Saturday morning including the main post at Calle Bon Aire 15, Maó.
Open: 9AM (Mon–Fri)
Closed: 2PM

ELECTRICITY

The power supply in Menorca is:
220–225 volts.

Sockets accept two-round-pin-style plugs, so an adaptor is needed for most non-Continental appliances and a transformer for appliances operating on 100–120 volts.

TIPS/GRATUITIES

Yes ✓ No ✗		
Restaurants (if service not included)	✓	10%
Cafés/bars	✓	change
Tour guides	✓	100ptas
Hairdressers	✓	100ptas
Taxis	✓	10%
Chambermaids	✓	100ptas
Porters	✓	100ptas
Theatre/cinema usherettes	✓	change
Cloakroom attendants	✓	change
Toilets	✗	

PHOTOGRAPHY

What to photograph: prehistoric monuments (*talayots*), secluded coves (*calas*), the old town areas of Maó and Ciutadella.

Best time to photograph: the Menorcan summer sun can be powerful at the height of the day making photos taken at this time appear 'flat'; it is best to photograph in the early morning or late evening.

Where to buy film: film and camera batteries are readily available from tourist shops and *drouguerías*.

HEALTH

Insurance
Nationals of EU and certain other countries can get medical treatment in Spain with the relevant documentation (Form E111 for Britons), although private medical insurance is still advised and is essential for all other visitors.

Dental Services
Dental treatment is not usually available free of charge as all dentists practice privately. A list of *dentistas* can be found in the yellow pages of the telephone directory. Dental treatment should be covered by private medical insurance.

Sun Advice
The sunniest (and hottest) months are July and August with an average of 11 hours sun a day and daytime temperatures of 29°C. Particularly during these months you should avoid the midday sun and use a strong sunblock.

Drugs
Prescription and non-prescription drugs and medicines are available from pharmacies (*farmàcias*), distinguished by a large green cross. They are able to dispense many drugs which would be available only on prescription in other countries.

Safe Water
Tap water is generally safe though it can be heavily chlorinated. Mineral water is cheap to buy and is sold as *con gaz* (carbonated) and *sin gaz* (still). Drink plenty of water during hot weather.

CONCESSIONS

Students Holders of an International Student Identity Card (ISIC) may be able to obtain some concessions on travel, entrance fees etc, but Menorca is not really geared up for students, it is more suited to families and senior citizens. There are no youth hostels, but for cheap accommodation the island's only official campsite S'Atalaia, just outside Cala Santa Galdana, is open all year (☎ 373095).

Senior Citizens Menorca is an excellent destination for older travellers, especially in winter when the resorts are quieter, prices more reasonable and hotels offer very economical long-stay rates. The best deals are available through tour operators who specialise in holidays for senior citizens.

CLOTHING SIZES

Menorca (Spain)	UK	Rest of Europe	USA	
46	36	46	36	Suits
48	38	48	38	
50	40	50	40	
52	42	52	42	
54	44	54	44	
56	46	56	46	
41	7	41	8	Shoes
42	7.5	42	8.5	
43	8.5	43	9.5	
44	9.5	44	10.5	
45	10.5	45	11.5	
46	11	46	12	
37	14.5	37	14.5	Shirts
38	15	38	15	
39/40	15.5	39/40	15.5	
41	16	41	16	
42	16.5	42	16.5	
43	17	43	17	
34	8	34	6	Dresses
36	10	36	8	
38	12	38	10	
40	14	40	12	
42	16	42	14	
44	18	44	16	
38	4.5	38	6	Shoes
38	5	38	6.5	
39	5.5	39	7	
39	6	39	7.5	
40	6.5	40	8	
41	7	41	8.5	

- Remember to contact the airport on the day prior to leaving to ensure the flight details are unchanged.
- If travelling by ferry you must check in no later than the time specified on the ticket.
- Spanish customs officials are usually polite and normally willing to negotiate.

LANGUAGE

The language that you hear on the streets is most likely to be Menorquín, a version of Catalan (Català), which itself shares features with both French and Spanish but sounds nothing like either and is emphatically a language, not a dialect. Catalan and Spanish both have official status on Menorca, and though Spanish will certainly get you by (it is still the language used by Menorcans to address strangers), it is useful to know some Catalan if only to understand all those street signs which are being slowly replaced in Catalan.

hotel	hotel	chambermaid	cambrera
bed and breakfast	llit i berenar	bath	bany
single room	habitació senzilla	shower	dutxa
double room	habitació doble	toilet	toaleta
one person	una persona	balcony	balcó
one night	una nit	key	clau
reservation	reservas	lift	ascensor
room service	servei d'habitació	sea view	vista al mar

bank	banc	credit card	carta de crèdit
exchange office	oficina de canvi	exchange rate	tant per cent
post office	correus	commission	comissió
coin	moneda	charge	
banknote	bitllet de banc	cashier	caixer
cheque	xec	change	camvi
traveller's cheque	xec de viatge	foreign currency	moneda estrangera

café	cafè	starter	primer plat
pub/bar	celler	main course	segón plat
breakfast	berenar	dessert	postres
lunch	dinar	bill	cuenta
dinner	sopar	beer	cervesa
table	mesa	wine	vi
waiter	cambrer	water	aigua
waitress	cambrera	coffee	café

aeroplane	avió	ticket	bitlet
airport	aeroport	single ticket	senzill-a
bus	autobús	return ticket	anar i tornar
station	estació	non-smoking	no fumar
bus stop	parada	car	cotxe
boat	vaixell	petrol	gasolina
port	port	how do I get to...?	per anar a...?
quay	moll	where is...?	on és...?

yes	sí	you're welcome	de res
no	no	how are you?	com va?
please	per favor	do you speak English?	parla anglès?
thank you	gràcies		
welcome	de res	I don't understand	no ho entenc
hello	hola		
goodbye	adéu	how much?	quant es?
good morning	bon dia	open	obert
good afternoon	bona tarda	closed	tancat
goodnight	bona nit	today	avui
excuse me	perdoni	tomorrow	demà

Acknowledgements
The Automobile Assocation wishes to thank the following libraries and photographers for their assistance in the preparation of this book:

IMAGES COLOUR LIBRARY F/c (a) building, Menorca
MARY EVANS PICTURE LIBRARY 10, 11
MRI BANKERS' GUIDE TO FOREIGN CURRENCY 119

The remaining photographs are held in the Association's own library (**AA PHOTO LIBRARY**) and were taken by James Tims.

Contributors
Copy editor: Rebecca Snelling **Page Layout:** Design 23 **Verifier:** Sheila Hawkins
Researcher (Practical Matters): Colin Follett **Indexer:** Marie Lorimer

Dear Essential Traveller

Your comments, opinions and recommendations are very important to us. So please help us to improve our travel guides by taking a few minutes to complete this simple questionnaire.

You do not need a stamp (unless posted outside the UK). If you do not want to cut this page from your guide, then photocopy it or write your answers on a plain sheet of paper.

Send to: **The Editor, AA World Travel Guides, FREEPOST SCE 4598, Basingstoke RG21 4GY.**

Your recommendations...

We always encourage readers' recommendations for restaurants, nightlife or shopping – if your recommendation is used in the next edition of the guide, we will send you a *FREE* AA *Essential* **Guide** of your choice. Please state below the establishment name, location and your reasons for recommending it.

_____
_____
_____
_____

Please send me **AA *Essential*** _____
(*see list of titles inside the front cover*)

About this guide...

Which title did you buy?
AA *Essential* _____
Where did you buy it? _____
When? m m / y y

Why did you choose an AA *Essential* Guide? _____
_____
_____
_____
_____

Did this guide meet your expectations?
Exceeded ☐ Met all ☐ Met most ☐ Fell below ☐
Please give your reasons _____
_____
_____
_____

continued on next page...

Were there any aspects of this guide that you particularly liked? _____

_____

_____

_____

Is there anything we could have done better? _____

_____

_____

_____

_____

About you...

Name (*Mr/Mrs/Ms*) _____

   Address _____

_____

_____ Postcode _____

   Daytime tel nos _____

Which age group are you in?
   Under 25 ☐   25–34 ☐   35–44 ☐   45–54 ☐   55–64 ☐   65+ ☐

How many trips do you make a year?
   Less than one ☐   One ☐   Two ☐   Three or more ☐

Are you an AA member? Yes ☐   No ☐

About your trip...

When did you book? m m / y y   When did you travel? m m / y y
How long did you stay? _____
Was it for business or leisure? _____
Did you buy any other travel guides for your trip?
   If yes, which ones? _____

_____

Thank you for taking the time to complete this questionnaire. Please send
   it to us as soon as possible, and remember, you do not need a stamp
   (*unless posted outside the UK*).

Happy Holidays!

The AA, its subsidiaries and any other companies or bodies in which it has an interest (the AA
Group) may use information about you to send you details of other products and services. The AA
Group as a matter of policy does not release its lists to third parties.
If you do not wish to receive further information please tick the box... ☐